Identity

To my family

Identity
Sociological perspectives

STEPH LAWLER

polity

First published in 2008 by Polity Press

Polity Press
65 Bridge Street
Cambridge CB2 1UR, UK.

Polity Press
350 Main Street
Malden, MA 02148, USA

ISBN-13: 978-07456-3575-0
ISBN-13: 978-07456-3576-7 (pb)

A catalogue record for this book is available from the British Library.

Typeset in 11 on 13 pt Scala
by Servis Filmsetting Ltd, Manchester
Printed and bound by Replika Press PVT Ltd, Kundli, India

The publisher has used its best endeavours to ensure that the URLs for external websites referred to in this book are correct and active at the time of going to press. However, the publisher has no responsibility for the websites and can make no guarantee that a site will remain live or that the content is or will remain appropriate.

Every effort has been made to trace all copyright holders, but if any have been inadvertently overlooked the publishers will be pleased to include any necessary credits in any subsequent reprint or edition.

For further information on Polity, visit our website: www.polity.co.uk

Contents

List of figures

Acknowledgements

Perhaps one of the most satisfying thing about finishing a book is being given the chance to acknowledge publicly all those small and large debts writers accrue throughout the course of a piece of work. So I'm very pleased to be able to feel I'm paying some debts, even though I know that ultimately they can't really be repaid.

This book was begun at Durham University and completed at Newcastle University. I would like to express my sincere appreciation of colleagues at both institutions. The initial idea for the book was that of Emma Longstaff at Polity, who persuaded me that I could do it and kept on persuading when I flagged. Thanks to Emma, who put an amazing amount of work into encouraging me to develop and improve the book, and to Philippa Youngman whose careful copy-editing considerably improved the manuscript.

The book grew out of a module, 'Self, Identity and Society', developed at Durham University by Robin Williams and myself. Thanks to all those who co-taught the module at various times: Becca Hazleden, Annie Meyer, Judy Richards and Robin Williams, who were wonderful colleagues. Thanks to students on the module, and on the 'Sociology of Identities' module at Newcastle, who have often been the unwitting interlocutors of developing ideas. More generally, thanks to all my undergraduate and postgraduate students at both Durham and Newcastle, who have been consistently inspiring.

Thanks to Karla Hackstaff for generously giving me permission to use her unpublished paper, 'Genealogy as social memory'. A longer version of chapter 7 was published as 'Disgusted subjects: the making of middle-class identities', in *The Sociological Review* (53, 3 (2005), 429–46). It is reproduced here by kind permission of *The Sociological Review*.

Special thanks to Mariam Fraser, Becca Hazleden, Paul Johnson and Ian Roberts, who were patient and generous enough to discuss many of the themes of the book; to Rose Griffiths and Toby Griffiths who, as ever, provided background music, love and humour; to Laura Higgins for the world's best cards and for steady encouragement. My greatest debt is to David Chaney, who not only encouraged and supported, but who read the entire manuscript under my gloomy gaze and, undeterred, came up with characteristically incisive and inspiring critiques.

This book is dedicated to my family, with thanks for all I have learned from them and all they have given me.

1 Introduction: identity as a question

'Identity' is a difficult term: more or less everyone knows more or less what it means, and yet its precise definition proves slippery. In popular culture, it tends to be explicitly invoked only when it is seen as 'being in trouble'. So we are accustomed to hear of 'identity crises', in which people are not quite sure who they are. Films such as *Identity* or *The Bourne Identity* signal its absence or its pathology. This might suggest that it only becomes important when it is missing, or otherwise a problem. And yet notions of identity are at the heart of many of the contemporary 'troubles' of Western[1] – and especially anglophone – cultures.

This book is about some of those troubles, and takes them as lenses through which to look at identity. It doing this, it considers how we might consider identities as being socially produced. That is, it considers how, through what mechanisms and in what ways, we can be said to achieve identity. As the title of the book implies, the perspectives taken here are sociological ones and the book has a specifically sociological approach to the issue of identity. This is about more than just offering a(nother) disciplinary perspective. Taking a sociological approach, I shall argue, enables the development of an expanded and fundamentally social and collective approach to identity, in contrast to the individualist and psychologistic perspectives that have tended to dominate discussions of this issue.

---

[1] I am using 'Western' here to designate what Marilyn Strathern calls 'Euro-American', which she uses to mean North American/northern European. More specifically, it refers to 'the largely middle-class, North American/Northern European discourse of public and professional life' (Strathern, 1996: 38). Language always fails us, I think, in these terms: obviously 'Western' is a conceptual rather than a geographic term. But I want to be careful to avoid a suggestion that the phenomena I discuss here are universal.

What is identity? sameness and difference

Part of the slipperiness of the term 'identity' derives from the difficulties of defining it adequately. It is not possible to provide a single,
overarching definition of what it is, how it is developed and how it
works. There are various ways of theorizing the concept, each of which
develops different kinds of definition. Thus it is not entirely possible
to answer the question, what is identity?, in advance of theorizing
about it. Each of the chapters will consider what identity means in the
context of particular modes of analysis.[2] However, it is useful, I think,
to give a very general, preliminary and contingent set of definitions at
this point.

The notion of identity hinges on an apparently paradoxical combination of sameness and difference. The root of the word 'identity' is
the Latin *idem* (same) from which we also get 'identical'. One important meaning of the term, then, rests on the idea that not only are we
identical with ourselves (that is, the same being from birth to death)
but we are identical with others. That is, we *share* common identities
– as humans, say, but also, within this, as 'women', 'men', 'British',
'American', 'white', 'black', etc. At the same time, however, there is
another aspect of identity, which suggests people's uniqueness, their
difference from others. Western notions of identity rely on these two
modes of understanding, so that people are understood as being
simultaneously the same and different. As Michael Jackson puts it,
people work with an awareness that 'one's humanity is simultaneously shared and singular' (Jackson, 2002: 142).

But within this overarching and apparently capacious category of
'the human', there are various forms of identity with which people
identify. Identity, then, involves *identification*. In identifying myself as
a woman, for example, I am identifying with a wider category,
'woman'. This overstates the case, of course: I may identify as a
woman at the same time as dis-identifying from certain features
of being a 'woman' that I find unattractive or unpalatable. I may
identify myself as a woman but be identified by others as something
else – as a man, perhaps, or a girl. But, although these processes are
complex, identifications are inevitably going on in processes of doing
identity.

[2] Throughout the book I also use terms such as 'person' and 'subject'. Such terms
are intended to be inclusive rather than technically exclusive, and are used in the
context of specific theoretical debates that, I hope, will unfold as the book pro-
gresses.

Furthermore, varying and often contradictory identities must be managed. No one has only one identity, in the sense that everyone must, consciously or not, identify with more than one group, one identity. This is about more than combining multiple identities in an 'additive' way. As several feminist writers have pointed out, identities impact on each other. It is not as though one could have a gendered identity, for example, and then, in addition to that, a raced identity, and then, somewhere 'on top of' that, a sexual identity and so on. Rather, race, gender and the rest interact (as do all forms of identity), so that to be a white woman is not the same – in terms of meaning or experience – as to be a black woman. Different forms of identity, then, should be seen as interactive and mutually constitutive, rather than 'additive'. They should also be seen as dynamic.

Some forms of identity, however, are understood to be mutually exclusive, and indeed rely on *not* being able to be combined. Examples include the binaries of man/woman, black/white, homosexual/heterosexual and so on. In these cases, identity categories are understood as being oppositional, and, in this context, identifications rely on their own *dis*-identifications. In identifying as a woman, one must reject an identification with the opposing category, 'man'. All identities are relational in this sense: all rely on *not* being something else. This is what Stuart Hall calls the 'constitutive outside' to identity. Hall argues,

> Throughout their careers, identities can function as points of identification and attachment only *because* of their capacity to exclude, to leave out, to render 'outside', abjected. Every identity has at its 'margin', an excess, something more. The unity, the internal homogeneity, which the term identity treats as foundational is not a natural, but a constructed form of closure, every identity naming as its necessary, even if silenced and unspoken other, that which it 'lacks' . . . So the 'unities' which identities proclaim are, in fact, constructed within the play of power and exclusion, and are the result, not of a natural and inevitable or primordial totality but of the naturalized, over-determined process of 'closure'. (Hall, 1996: 5, emphasis in original)

So, one threat to the notion of a stable, coherent self – its 'internal homogeneity' – is the recognition that no one has only one identity; and indeed those identities may be in tension (one example would be the ways in which 'mother' and 'worker' are often understood as existing in tension). A second threat comes in the recognition that identities, equally, rely on the expulsion of what they are not. And yet, if we return to the concept of a common humanity, discussed earlier, what is going on here? Why are identities asserted within this category of 'humanity'?

One answer to this question is that identities are asserted because people have 'obvious' differences: and yet differences are not necessarily at all obvious – although this does not stop blood being shed in their name. So wars and conflicts between Serbs, Croats and Bosnians in the former Yugoslavia, between Hutu and Tutsi in Rwanda, between Catholics and Protestants in Northern Ireland, and many other conflicts – all have relied on the precept that there are fundamental differences in identity between different groups. Yet these differences are not simply 'there'; they are not 'given in nature' but need to be *made* (see Ignatieff, 1994). In similar ways, the distinction of Nazi race laws had to be made, and the German government of the 1930s and 1940s had to go to great lengths to determine, for example, who was and who was not Jewish.

Several commentators, following Freud (1918), have termed this creation of difference 'the narcissism of small differences'. In wanting to see ourselves as unique, we magnify small differences until they become defining characteristics. What is shared is played down, what is different is played up, until identities come to seem 'opposites'. This is clearly the case with ethnic or 'racial' differences, such as those mentioned above, since there is no real, objective difference between the different groups, and 'race', it is now generally agreed, refers not to an 'objective fact of nature' but to divisions made within racism. What gets to count as racial difference, in other words, is whatever racism makes into those differences. Sexual difference is frequently understood as being objectively marked by bodily difference, but, here too, small differences are made into defining characteristics, such that two sexes become 'opposites'. As Gayle Rubin comments,

> In fact, from the standpoint of nature, men and women are closer to each other than either is to anything else – for instance, mountains, kangaroos or coconut palms . . . though there is an average difference between males and females in a variety of traits, the range of variation of those traits shows a considerable overlap . . . [E]xclusive gender identity . . . requires repression, in men, of whatever is the local version of 'feminine' traits; in women of the local version of 'masculine' traits. (Rubin, 1975: 179–80)

So too with other forms of apparently 'natural' and 'obvious' differences.

What is being suggested here is that what is similar must be suppressed to produce differences that come to seem so obvious and 'natural'. As we shall see in the Afterword, the extreme form of this move results in expelling certain people or groups of people even from the category 'human'. In the next section, however, I want to consider the notion of 'uniqueness' in identity and to consider what this uniqueness might consist in, and what might be suppressed to make it, in turn, seem of overriding significance.

'I am who I am': the unique kernel of identity?

If, as I have argued, identity turns on both sameness and uniqueness, what is it that makes each of us unique? One answer might be that nobody has exactly the same life: even siblings – even identical twins – do not share every aspect of life. But, more commonly, uniqueness is seen as something which belongs to the person in question and is nothing to do with the social world. The social world might impact upon it and shape it, but (it is generally assumed) it does not make it. What the 'it' in question is depends on the position taken. In some versions, it might be a unique combination of genes; in others, it is a 'soul'. In every case, though, that posits some notion of some part of a person that is not produced by the social world, what is being posited is an essence: something that makes the person what she or he is. It is often seen as what lies 'inside', and is understood as being 'deeper' or 'truer' than what is 'outside'. So although Western persons are probably comfortable with the idea that the social world produces *part of* who they are, and indeed with the idea that who they are can and will change, this is often accompanied by a notion of a 'true' or 'deep' self, which is seen as somehow outside all the social.

I would not want to deny that, in important ways, everyone is different, but I do want to question the assumption that this difference inheres within a core which is outside the social world. I also want to consider how such beliefs come to be so strong, and to consider, too, what work such an assumption does – that is, what are its effects?

The book as a whole represents my attempt to address these questions, but it is worth at this point highlighting what I see as the importance of such an enquiry for sociology. Norbert Elias (1994) has argued that it is impossible to have a satisfactory sociology of persons while seeing 'the individual' or some part of the individual as standing outside 'society'. Elias recognizes that there is a widespread *perception* that one's 'true identity' is somehow 'locked away inside', and that one is a bounded, self-contained individual. He is concerned, however, to question whether this perception is an adequate foundation for analysis;

after all, if we relied on perception as an adequate decider of truth, we would be left with the view that the sun does indeed go round the earth. For Elias, this view of a true, 'inner core' is so taken for granted that questions are rarely asked of it. As a result identity becomes a 'black box', unknown and unknowable, and this is true for social scientific knowledge (including sociology) as well as for literary representations and generalized 'lay' assumptions. Elias writes,

> The question is whether this self-perception, and the image of man [sic] in which it is usually crystallized quite spontaneously and without reflection, can serve as a reliable starting point for an attempt to gain adequate understanding of human beings . . . Is it justified – that is the question – to place at the foundation of philosophical theories of perception and knowledge, and of sociological and other theories in the human sciences, as a self-evident assumption incapable of further explanation, the sharp dividing line between what is 'inside' man and the 'external world', a division which often appears directly given in self-awareness, and furthermore has put down deep roots in European intellectual and linguistic traditions, without a critical and systematic examination of its validity? (Elias, 1994: 206)

Instead of starting with this perception, as – as he rightly notes – sociologists had done until relatively recently, Elias starts with the social conditions that give rise to the perception. In other words, instead of taking the perception of a unique inner core to be the basis on which the social world works, he asks what it is about the culture and history of the social world that has given rise to such a widespread belief and perception.

For Elias, this notion of an 'inner' 'hidden' core to the self, experienced as 'inside' (even if we could not quite say what is the border between 'inside' and 'outside'), is not an inevitable feature of the human condition but a consequence of what he famously calls 'the civilizing process' in the West. This process – from about the time of the Renaissance – involved increasing emphases on notions of self-control. Manners must be observed; people ought not to act on sensory or other bodily impulses. In important senses, for Elias, manners make the person; that is, Western persons *became* self-controlled beings as a result of injunctions to self-control. This notion of the need to manage 'internal' states has led to a perception of 'true identity' being contained 'inside', while the social world is firmly 'outside':

> What is encapsulated are the restrained instinctual and affective impulses denied direct access to the motor apparatus. They appear in self-perception

as what is hidden from all others, and often as the true self, the core of individuality. (Elias, 1994: 211)

So, for Elias, the notion that the 'true self' or a 'true identity' is 'inside', and is fundamentally separated from the social world, is an effect, not of any innate feature of human identity itself, but from social processes of (self-)control. In turn, the notion has become reified so that it has become a feature of various modes of understanding identity.

What follows from this? For one thing, a 'black box' approach to identity has meant that identity has, until relatively recently, been seen as not amenable to sociological study. That is, if identity is locked away 'inside' – and, furthermore, if it exists outside the social world, why should sociologists study it? The fact that this book exists at all is of course an indication of changes that have occurred here, but it is still possible to encounter the view that the study of identity is somehow outside the real business of sociology – that 'real business' having conventionally, and with certain important exceptions, revolved around the study of 'large-scale' social structures. But can the person and the social world really be separated in this way? Mariam Fraser comments,

[C]lass inequalities, which might be thought of as 'large scale' issues of social and economic justice (or injustice), give rise to 'real' social effects, one of which is classed subjectivities. (Fraser, 1999: 120)

So too with other forms of 'large-scale' justice or injustice. These 'systemic' processes inflict what Sennett and Cobb have called 'hidden injuries' (Sennett and Cobb, 1977). Far from identities being formed in opposition to the social world they are, as I shall argue throughout this book, formed *by* the social world. While sociology ignores questions of identity, seeing them as outside, or nothing to do with, the social, or as coming fully formed into the social world, one effect is the curious situation of a sociology which represses the social when it comes to the business of how identities get produced.

This 'inner/outer' split identified by Elias also has other effects, one of them being to mask human interdependency. As Elias notes, Westerners are accustomed to thinking of themselves as their own little self-enclosed world – *homo clausus*, as he terms it. But – and as I suggested above – this process involves the suppression of an alternative perception, one which understands the person in terms of their relations with others, and hence understands identity as formed *between*, rather than *within* persons. This view, to quote Elias again, conceptualizes the person as being

[F]undamentally oriented toward and dependent on other people through-out his [sic] life. The network of interdependencies between human beings is what binds them together. Such interdependencies are the nexus of what is here called the figuration, a structure of mutually oriented and dependent people . . . [People] exist, one might venture to say, only as plur-alities, only as figurations. (Elias, 1994: 213–14)

'Without you I'm nothing': without a nexus of others, none of us could be 'who we are'. The Western notion of the individual, however, rests on a massive suppression of this complex interdependency and suggests a model of identity which is, at its heart, outside the social world. As Elias suggests, sociological analysis has to challenge this notion, rather than incorporating it.

About the book

Following on from this, the central claim of this book is that identity needs to be understood not as belonging 'within' the individual person, but as produced between persons and within social relations. Its overall aim is to consider some of the ways in which identity can be understood sociologically. This is not because all the perspectives I discuss here are from the discipline of sociology, but because, I believe, they all throw sociological light on the topic of identity. They enable us to think about identity as socially produced, socially embed-ded and worked out in people's everyday social lives.

I referred at the start of this chapter to contemporary 'troubles' that cohere around identity. These will be discussed throughout the book and include (but are not limited to) a concern with memory, history and storytelling; a concern with sameness and difference in relation to others; a concern with the government of private life and the main-tenance of a moral order; a concern with the limits of agency; and a concern with authenticity. I shall suggest that these troubles tell us a great deal about when identities are seen to go 'wrong'. As a result, they tell us about what the 'right' identities are held to be like. 'Identity talk', sometimes explicitly but more usually implicitly, is about the 'ought' rather than the 'is' of identities.

The book opens with a consideration of the significance of memory, history and storytelling: chapter 2 discusses the role of narratives and stories in the production of identities, and, specifically, the relation-ship between 'life' and 'story' through the notion of narrative identity. Chapter 3 analyses identity in the context of kinship. In the face of a considerable emphasis on a decline in the significance of kinship,

I argue that it remains an important way in which Westerners conceptualize their identities. Chapter 4 considers identity as a project to be worked on. It examines the argument that one important way in which people in the West have come to be governed is precisely through this project of the self – through the self working on itself. Chapter 5 turns to questions of the unconscious and asks how far subjectivities are the products of unknown, unconscious motivations: the hidden desires, fears and envies that are theorized within psychoanalysis. In chapter 6 I discuss whether and to what extent identity can be seen in terms of a performance – not because it is 'false' but because that is precisely how even truthful forms of identity get to be done. I then turn, in chapter 7, to one particular form of identity politics as I examine how middle-class identities can be seen to be formulated on the basis of a repudiation of working-class identities that are themselves seen as being founded on the basis of a lack of 'taste'. I end the book by returning to the concept of 'identity ties' and considering how the suppression of ties between self and other can be linked with ideas of value: who does, and who does not, have a worthwhile, a valuable, identity?

This book is partial in two senses: it gives only a partial analysis of identity. It does not attempt to cover every perspective on identity, or to give a comprehensive overview of the theorists discussed here. Rather, it aims to consider a number of ways in which identity might be thought sociologically, in the context of some issues that seem to be troubling in the contemporary world. I have tried to show how the perspectives discussed can be 'good to think with'. The book is also partial in concentrating largely on one time – the contemporary – and one place, or rather, on one set of people – largely, those living in North America and Europe and who are generally designated 'Western'. To paraphrase Pierre Bourdieu, this is not because I am 'Western' (although I am) but because this is the time and place I have studied. As well, the book is partial in that it is not impartial. It is not disinterested but argues for the theoretical and political salience of identity, and for a sociology that problematizes and investigates this difficult yet important notion.

2 Stories, memories, identities

Introduction: living lives and telling stories

Let me start this chapter on stories with a story.

> **Gina:** My mother was very much one of those working-class mothers, where you don't play in the house. You know, the house has got to be kept clean. You play outside. Your friends don't come into the house and mess the house up. Er, you don't have people round for tea, unless it's something special, or they're your relations . . . She would always get very nervous if visitors came, you know. Everything would have to be just so. . . . So I had it in my head, when I decided that I wanted children, that . . . I wanted to have people in and out all the time. Lots of life, lots of different kinds of people, lots of different influences, different ages. You know, *life* in the house . . . I wanted to live in a big rambly house. I wanted a big garden, you know. I wanted there to be trees, somewhere the kids could play. I suppose I had middle-class aspirations for my kids. I wanted them to be a bit like the Famous Five[1] [laughs]. I wanted them to have sort of adventures, and dogs, and, you know, erm, sort of paddle in streams . . . I wanted the skies always to be blue, and the sun to shine, and I wanted to make jam and cakes and bread and do all those things. And then I did sort of try to do that when I came to live [here]. (Emphasis hers)

This fragment of a larger narrative[2] is taken from research I did on the mother–daughter relationship (Lawler, 2000). This particular extract is taken from one of four interviews with Gina,[3] a woman in her 40s, recounting here the difference between her own style of

---

[1] The Famous Five are a group of four white, middle-class children and a dog (Timmy) who feature in a series of books written between the 1940s and the 1960s by the English children's author, Enid Blyton.

[2] There is some debate about whether stories and narratives are the same thing: nevertheless, I use 'stories' and 'narratives' more or less interchangeably throughout the chapter since, for the purposes of this argument, they do the same work.

[3] A pseudonym.

mothering, and that of her mother. Although brief, and apparently straightforward, it is rich with meaning, as Gina uses a range of cultural symbols to tell her story. I include it here as an illustration of much of what I want to discuss in this chapter about the stories, or narratives, we tell, and the ways in which they are linked with identity and, indeed, with the ways in which identities can be understood as being made through narratives.

What is the connection between this brief story of (part of) Gina's life, and Gina's identity? One way of reading the narrative would be to see it as reflecting a process of developing an identity which occurs quite independently of the narrative. An alternative way of seeing it, however, is to see Gina as engaged in processes of *producing* an identity through assembling various memories, experiences, episodes, etc. within narrative. It is this latter way of understanding identity that I will explore in this chapter. That is, I am concerned here to consider identities as 'made up' through making a *story* out of a *life*. In describing identities as 'made up' in this way, let me stress that I am not suggesting they are fabricated in the normal sense of the word (as in 'falsified'). I want, rather, to suggest that identities can be seen as being creatively produced through various raw materials available – notably, memories, understandings, experiences and interpretations. I will return to all of these issues.

Gina's narrative has the three components which Paul Ricoeur – upon whose work I will draw throughout this chapter – identifies as being crucial to narratives: characters, action and plot. That is, narratives are accounts that must minimally contain characters (human and/or non-human), action (movement through time, including transformation) and plot. The plot is a central feature of narrative: it is, fundamentally, what *makes* the narrative, in that it brings together different events and episodes into a meaningful whole: events or episodes are not thrown together at random, but are linked together. Both the narrator and the audience will participate in the processes of linking – which Ricoeur calls 'emplotment' – through a shared cultural understanding that *these* events have a place in *this* narrative. Above all, what narratives like Gina's, here, convey is the story of the production of an identity. As Carolyn Steedman has observed, it is 'always the same story in the end, that is the individual's account of how she got to be the way she is' (Steedman, 1986: 132).

Gina's narrative has two principal characters – herself and her mother, although it also includes her imagined children and her real children. Although it largely centres on her desires, these desires are narrated as being linked to episodes: her mother's tidiness and lack of sociability, Gina's desire for (and eventual achievement of) an entirely different lifestyle. There is action (movement through time and transformation) as Gina narrates the origins and the consummation of her desires. We get a glimpse of Gina the child in the narrative of Gina the adult – a narrative which is told 'backwards' from the present time. The events she narrates are not simply random occurrences: they have a place in the plot and so they *produce* the narrative, which is, as I suggested above, a narrative of how Gina got to be the way she is. She does not have to signal this explicitly: it is already written into our broader cultural understanding of narratives.

The narrative cannot stand alone but must refer to and draw on wider cultural narratives. Although they are largely implicit here, narratives about how class impacts on living arrangements, about working-class respectability and a kind of 'alternative' middle-class existence are nevertheless present. As I have already noted, Gina uses a range of cultural symbols, including fictional narratives (the Famous Five) to narrate her movement through time. These symbols 'work' in the narrative because they are understood culturally as signifying more than themselves. 'Big rambly houses' and children who have adventures like the Famous Five signify a particular kind of classed existence. In constituting those symbols in particular configurations, she is engaged in the creative work of imposing a unity on her identity, yet this unity is, as Lois McNay has observed in relation to narrative identity more generally, 'the dynamic unity of change through time' (McNay, 2000: 75). Read in this way, Gina's identity can be seen as being produced through a series of creative acts in which she interprets and reinterprets her memories and experiences, articulated within narrative.

Indeed, such narratives, or stories, can be seen as basic to Western culture, as to many – perhaps all – cultures, although of course what counts as a good or reasonable story varies historically and cross-culturally. As Barbara Hardy (1975) has observed, we could hardly live without telling stories, both to others and to ourselves. We wake to fragments of dream-stories, we go to sleep after retelling much of the day to ourselves, and at various points in between we are engaged in processes of recounting and telling, to ourselves and to others, what has passed and what we hope will pass. We endlessly tell stories about our lives, both to ourselves and to others; and it is through such stories that we make sense of the world, of our relationship to that world and of the relationship between ourselves and other selves:

The stories of our days and the stories in our days are joined in that auto-biography we are all engaged in making and remaking, as long as we live, which we never complete, though we all know how it is going to end. (Hardy, 1975: 4)

These stories are not simple acts of description but are complicated procedures for making sense of the world, of the details of our days and, ultimately of our lives. They are interpretive devices through which people make sense of, understand and live their lives.

As I noted in relation to Gina's story, from a narrative perspective the relationship between identity and autobiography is not that autobiography (the telling of a life) *reflects* a pre-given identity: rather, identities are *produced* through the autobiographical work in which all of us engage every day, even though few of us will formally write an 'autobiography'. The narratives we produce in this context are stories of how we come to be the way we are. But it is *through* the narratives themselves that we produce our identities in this way. This revolves around *interpretation*. Henrietta Moore argues that 'narrative is a strategy for placing us within a historically constituted world . . . If narrative makes the world intelligible, it also makes ourselves intelligible' (Moore, 1994: 119). Lynne Segal expresses something similar in her comment that

Our own most cherished conceits, stubborn evasions or persistent illu-sions are all fashioned by a growing stock of cultural narratives, as we try to make sense of the past and its connections to our lives in the present. This . . . is what we need to study, not seek to evade. (Segal, 1999: 118)

In the rest of this chapter I shall trace the development of narrative as the focus of sociological inquiry before considering narrative's sig-nificance in terms of identity-formation. I shall suggest that narrative gives us a means to understand identity in its sociality, since narrative identity places us within a complex web of relationships and, ulti-mately, confounds the notion of the atomized individual.

Sociological thinking about narratives

Conventionally, the study of narratives has been rooted in literary criticism and has tended to be concerned with the technical elements of the narrative structure. However, there is a relatively long, if some-what marginal, tradition of sociological thought which has attended to narratives. This includes William Dilthey's nineteenth-century call for a 'sociology of biography' (see Dilthey, 1976), through the Chicago School's (twentieth-century) research which elicited individual biographical accounts, and on to more recent 'life history' and auto/biographical research and research which considers whole or partial narratives in the more direct context of identity production. In the last fifteen or so years, however, a focus on narrative has intensified within sociological and other social-science analyses. A number of developments – not least a concern with identity itself – can be seen to be behind this intensification. Stanley and Morgan (1993), in their consideration of auto/biography within sociology, argue that recent attention to it is part of a rethinking of intellectual inquiry (including, but not exclusively, sociological inquiry). They identify five characteristics which, they argue, provide the background to this attention to auto/biography: first, a turn to textuality, in which written texts are seen as *social products*, rather than as unproblematic and transparent reflections of social reality; second, a questioning of the sharp distinction between structure and agency, and between individual and collective action; and third, an examination of what they call 'referentiality and lives' – in other words, an attention to questions about the relationship between representations of lives, and the lives themselves, and between descriptions of all kinds and the events they describe. Fourth, they argue, an increasing attention to *time* has been significant. This focus has drawn attention, for example, to the ways in which, in telling a life, certain periods are compressed in favour of others. It also draws attention to the ways in which memory works through selective processes, heightening the significance of some time periods and diminishing the significance of others. Finally, they see a turn to intertextuality as significant: in producing a life story (one sort of text) we are always, implicitly or explicitly, referring to and drawing on other texts – other life stories, fictional and non-fictional, as well as a range of different kinds of texts. This should not be taken to suggest that the resulting narrative is 'false', but simply that, in telling a life, people are simultaneously interpreting that life. Narrative analysis is embedded within a hermeneutic tradition of inquiry in that it is concerned with understanding: how people understand and make sense of their lives, and how analysts can understand that understanding (Lawler, 2008).

What is a narrative?

As I noted above, narrative must contain action or transformation and characters, which must be brought together within an overall plot. For Paul Ricoeur, the central element of a narrative is its plot. Plots are not, as it were, taken off the shelf. Instead, they are *produced within the work of narrative.* A plot only *becomes* a plot through the active work of emplotment. Emplotment connects. Ricoeur defines emplotment, at its most basic, as 'a synthesis of heterogeneous elements' (1991a: 21). Disparate things are brought together, as in Gina's narrative, which brings together elements which don't inevitably or automatically go together – tidy and untidy houses, mothering, jam making and the Famous Five – into one coherent story. Ricoeur elaborates three main (and overlapping) forms of synthesis at work in emplotment.

1   **The synthesis between many events and one story.** In this context, an event is more than simply something that happens: it must have a part in the story, contributing to the progress of the narrative. It must contribute to the coherence and intelligibility of the narrative.

2   **The synthesis between discordance and concordance.** In other words, the plot both incorporates quite disparate events and episodes, unintended consequences, and so on, and functions as a totality: one story.

3   **The synthesis between two different senses of time**: time, on the one hand, as open and indefinite, embedded in a series of successive incidents (so that we ask of a story, 'and then? and then?') and time as something closed and 'over with'. As Ricoeur puts it, 'time is both what passes and flows away and, on the other hand, what endures and remains' (1991a: 22).

The central point here is that it is emplotment which makes an account a narrative. It is emplotment which turns disparate events into 'episodes' (Somers and Gibson, 1994) which have a part in the beginning, the end and the movement of a plot. Even if the events seem unrelated they will be brought together through the overall coherence of the plot. In other words, not everything is narrated (to ourselves or to others). The events, desires and so on that *are* narrated must have some significance for the overall 'plot'. Furthermore, they are *given* significance by being incorporated into the plot. Readers or hearers of narrative will tend to assume some meaning: they will engage in active interpretation. If I relate the story of a happy and indulged childhood, you may infer that certain negative or positive character traits are made explicable by means of that narrative (this is much more likely to occur with happiness than with misery, since as I argue below there is a premium put on misery). Equally, you may believe that I am self-deluded or engaging in defensiveness and that my childhood was less happy and indulged than I present it. In any case, you will interpret my narrative. The narrative, then, is only completed (if it ever is!) in the interaction between teller and audience.

But the initial narrative is *itself* both an interpretation and the creative assemblage of disparate elements. It is an interpretation because I do not have unmediated access to the 'self who was' (Stanley, 1992). I am constructing earlier events from memories, but I am both interpreting those memories and engaging in a larger interpretation in selecting which events will make up a particular story. That is, out of the millions of things that occur in a life, only some will be selected as 'events' with which to construct a story. And those that are selected will be chosen precisely because the narrator sees them as having a *point* within the story. Further, narrated events will be *given* a significance in becoming part of the narrative. The various elements that make up the plot must be selected and then put together so that they have some point. In relation to narrative identity, the various events of the life story must be narrated so that they have some point in explaining how the narrator came to be the person she or he is.

Within narratives, and through processes of emplotment, prior events seem *inevitably* to lead to later ones, and the end of the story is understood as the culmination and actualization of prior events. Significance is conferred on earlier events by what comes later. In this sense, narratives become naturalized as the episodes which make up the 'plot' appear inevitable, and even universal. The end of a story does not have to be predictable, but it must be meaningful. In short, a narrative must have a *point*; as both Paul Ricoeur (1980) and Carolyn Steedman (1986) have pointed out, the question every narrator tries to fend off is, 'so what?'. And for narratives to have a point, they must incorporate this important element of bringing together disparate elements into a single plot:

> The connectivity of parts is precisely why narrativity turns 'events' into episodes, whether the sequence of episodes is presented or experienced in anything resembling chronological or categorical order. And it is emplotment which translates events into episodes. As a mode of explanation, causal emplotment is an accounting (however fantastic or implicit) of why a narrative has the story line it does. (Somers and Gibson, 1994: 58)

Narrative (and) identity

Emplotment configures a self which appears as the inevitable outcome and actualization of the episodes which constitute a life. The self is understood as unfolding through episodes which both express and constitute that self. The very constitution of an identity is configured over time and through narrative.

According to this perspective, then, identity is profoundly social, and is continually interpreted and reinterpreted. Insofar as we know ourselves (and others), we achieve this knowledge only though interpretation. Ricoeur writes,

> [T]he self does not know itself immediately but only indirectly by the detour of the cultural signs of all sorts which are articulated on the symbolic mediations which always already articulate action and, among them, the narratives of everyday life. Narrative mediation underlines this remarkable characteristic of self-knowledge – that it is self-interpretation. (Ricoeur, 1991b: 198)

So identity is not something foundational and essential, but something *produced* through the narratives people use to explain and understand their lives. We tend to see the self as continuing as the same thing through time, and to see this as deriving from some characteristic(s) of the self itself. But, for Ricoeur, the reason we see the self in this way is because we constantly tell and retell stories which *produce* it as something continuing through time.

In narrating a story, social actors organize events into 'episodes' which make up the plot. In doing so, of course, they draw on memories. But, not only do they interpret those memories, the memories are *themselves* interpretations. It is not simply that memory is unreliable (although it is): the point is that memories are themselves social products. What we remember depends on the social context. As Barbara Misztal (2003) has observed, memory is reconstructive. And Ian Hacking comments,

> Memory is not like a video record. It does not need images, and images are never enough: moreover, our memories shade and patch and combine and delete . . . [T]he best analogy to remembering is storytelling . . . We constitute our souls by making up our lives, that is, by weaving stories about our past, by what we call memories. The tales we tell of ourselves and to ourselves are not a matter of recording what we have done and how we have felt. They must mesh with the rest of the world and with other people's stories, at least in externals, but their real role is the creation of a life, a character. (Hacking, 1995: 250–1)

As a demonstration of the reconstructive, interpretive character of memory, Misztal cites an experiment carried out by Frederic Bartlett in 1932. In this experiment, white US college students were asked to read a Native American legend and then to recall the story as accurately as possible. Bartlett found that the students tended to forget those parts of the story that did not fit their cultural framework or expectations. Misztal comments,

> Frames of meaning, or ways in which we view the past, are generated in the present and usually match the group's common view of the world . . . We rely on them to supply us with what we should remember and what is taboo, and therefore must be forgotten. (Misztal, 2003: 82; see also Prager, 2000)

We must constantly engage in recall, retelling, interpretation, in order to conjure up the past; we must engage in what Ian Hacking (1994; 1995) has called 'memoro-politics' – a process by which the past is interpreted in the light of the knowledge and understanding of the subject's 'present'. As Steedman puts it,

> We all return to memories and dreams . . . again and again; the story we tell of our life is reshaped around them. But the point doesn't lie there, back in the past, back in the lost time at which they happened; the only point lies in interpretation. The past is re-used through the agency of social information, and that interpretation of it can only be made with what people know of a social world and their place within it. (Steedman, 1986: 5)

There is no unmediated access to the 'facts of the matter', nor to a straightforward and unmediated 'experience'. As the past is remembered, it is interpreted and reinterpreted in the light of the person's knowledge and understanding. Liz Stanley points up this gap between past and present in her analysis of auto/biography; she argues,

> [T]he 'self who writes' has no more direct and unproblematic access to the 'self who was' than does the reader; and anyway 'the autobiographical past' is actually peopled by a succession of selves as the writer grows, develops and changes. (Stanley, 1992: 61)

What we make of 'experience' depends on what we know about the ways in which those experiences relate to the wider social circumstances of our lives. Although this is, inevitably, a post hoc treatment, the events of a life come to appear as though naturally and inevitably leading to their specific conclusion. We 'read time backwards', as Ricoeur puts it, 'reading the end into the beginning and the beginning into the end' (Ricoeur, 1980: 183), interpreting later events in the light of earlier ones, and interpreting the self in terms of the emplotment of events:

Memory . . . is itself the spiral movement that, through anecdotes and episodes, brings us back to the almost motionless constellation of potentialities that the narrative retrieves. The end of the story is what equates the present with the past, the actual with the potential. The hero *is* who he [*sic*] *was*. (Ricoeur, 1980: 186, emphasis in original)

Narrative, then, suggests movement through time – the movement from the potential to the actual, from what could be to what is, from past to present, from present to future. In the process, it works to *naturalize* the plot, making later events seem the natural and inevitable culmination of earlier ones. But what looks like a natural, causal relationship is, according to Ricoeur, a teleological one; that is, the episodes which make up the plot are there because of the purpose they serve (which is *to produce* a coherent plot): 'Looking back from the conclusion to the episodes leading up to it, we have to be able to say that this ending required these sorts of events and this chain of actions' (Ricoeur, 1980: 174).

That this seems like an effect of the life rather than the story is an effect of seeing narratives precisely as transparent carriers of a 'true life'. As we have seen, this is inadequate since there are always processes of interpretation going on. Søren Kierkegaard observed that 'life is lived forwards but understood backwards' (in Geertz, 1995), but it might be better to see life as being both lived and understood forwards *and* backwards in a 'spiral movement' of constant interpretation and reinterpretation. People constantly produce and reproduce life stories on the basis of memories, interpreting the past through the lens of social information, and using this information to formulate present and future life stories. Narrative provides a means of conceptualizing people in the context of history: if the past is always interpreted through the present, then, equally, this (interpreted) past informs the present.

Self and other

By considering identity in terms of narrative, it is possible to see past and present linked in a spiral of interpretation and reinterpretation. It is possible, also, to break down the dividing line between self and other and thus to see selves and identities as embedded in the social world. A focus on narrative challenges the concept of the atomized individual and replaces it with a concept of a person enmeshed in – and produced within – webs of social relations. This is for two major reasons: first, because life stories (identity-narratives) must always incorporate the life stories of others. They will not be the same as those others' stories; they will always be particular versions, but nevertheless others' stories must always be part of our own. One can imagine, taking Gina's narrative, above, that her mother would have told a different story about the transformations in Gina's life: Gina's narrative is not her mother's, yet both are enmeshed. Furthermore, others' stories sometimes provide the basis for our own, as intimates furnish parts of stories that have been forgotten, or (as in the case of early childhood) furnish the stories themselves. Even memory itself – which is conventionally understood as being 'owned' by the individual – can be seen as being produced in complex, intersubjective relationships. Jeffrey Prager, for example, writes of 'the ways in which the cultural and the interpersonal interpenetrate in memory, a process generally thought to be purely individual', and argues that memories are 'the result of an individual's relation to both self and the outside world' (2000: 59–60).

Second, the social world can *itself* be seen as storied, in that, as Somers and Gibson put it,

> [S]tories guide action; . . . people construct identities (however multiple and changing) by locating themselves or being located within a repertoire of emplotted stories; . . . 'experience' is constituted through narratives; . . . people make sense of what has happened and is happening to them by attempting to assemble or in some way to integrate these happenings within one or more narratives; and . . . people are guided to act in certain ways, and not others, on the basis of the projections, expectations, and memories derived from a multiplicity but ultimately linked repertoire of available social, public and cultural narratives. (Somers and Gibson, 1994: 38–9)

If the social world is always storied, it puts constraints on the stories we produce, since our own narratives of identity would simply not make sense if they did not accord with broader 'intelligibility norms'. Gina's narrative, for example, only makes sense in a time and place in which we understand mothering as significant, if not decisive, in terms of how the child (and especially the daughter) turns out, in which we associate certain ways of living with certain class milieux, and so on. Our social milieu also provides a set of *resources* on which we can draw to produce our own stories. There are, for example, the plots provided by the literary tradition, but narratives are also provided by soap operas, 'expert' advice, talk shows and so on. Ricoeur argues that through using existing narratives we create our own – in which we are the heroes of our own lives. We are not, however, the authors of these stories since they do not originate with us: in effect, we are putting various facets of narrative traditions together to produce our 'own' story and hence our 'own' narrative. Various forms of narrative become resources on which we can draw in constituting our own narrative identity. Indeed, as Nikolas Rose (1999) points out, the rationale behind the teaching of literature in schools was the belief that children ought to learn to reflect on their inner lives and inner selves – and that they should learn this by identifying with characters in novels. Carolyn Steedman (1996) points to a somewhat different, though overlapping, set of resources – those of history. What she suggests is that, in learning to identify with other people, other events and other times, we are learning specific ways to reflect on and understand ourselves. And in this, we make our life stories in particular ways, we marshal our memories in particular ways, we make sense of experience in specific ways – in other words, we assemble sets of 'episodes' to make an ongoing story and within this story we are able to say 'that is me', 'I am like this'.

Steedman argues that history provides a particularly compelling set of resources. She sees history in terms of ideation – a way of thinking, rather than a collection of 'facts'. For Steedman, history is a particular way of conceptualizing the world that came into being in Europe around the end of the seventeenth century. As a way of seeing and conceptualizing the world, then, history is not a set of (objective) historical 'facts' that stands apart from memory and personal testimony; rather, 'formal history' provides a way of understanding not only the 'public' collective world, but also one's place within it as an individual and one's own personal history. As Steedman puts it, 'loosed upon the world, the protocols of formal history become components of memory, of verbal narrative, of misremembering' (1996: 109).

What this suggests is that 'history' as a way of seeing and understanding the world becomes a resource to use when thinking about and constituting our own life histories. In the process, it becomes a resource in constituting narrative identities. Indeed, for Steedman, in Britain at least (but no doubt much further afield also) we are enjoined to understand history through processes of identification. A post-war educational system has encouraged students learning history at every level to 'find themselves in the text': to understand through identifying with 'something (someone, some group, some series of events)' (Steedman, 1996: 103). But this is a two-way movement, since it is not simply that 'the individual' reflects on history, but that one's very identity is produced, at least in part, through ways of understanding identity that have been given to us by history:

In the project of finding an identity through the processes of historical identification, the past is searched for something (someone, some group, some series of events) that confirms the searcher in his or her sense of self, confirms them as they want to be and feel in some measure that they already are. The search is for all the ideas, and times, and images, that will give us, now, solidity and meaning in time. (Steedman, 1996: 103)

Identifying with: the subjects of pain

So far, I have presented the argument that identities are dynamic, that they are produced through narratives, that such narrative identities link self and other, and past and present, and that processes of identification are increasingly important in terms of how people produce their identities. In this section I want to discuss what might be seen as the other side of this identification; I want to ask, what kinds of pitfalls are there on the road to establishing an identity through identifying with another?

For Steedman, as we have seen, identities are produced through complex processes through which we identify with an other – in which, as it were, people put themselves into someone else's story, and, in the process and through processes of reworking, make it their *own* story. Steedman (1986) suggests that this urge to be part of a story – even if it is someone else's, even if one doesn't quite fit – is extremely strong. In her later work, Steedman turns to specific ways in which identification with a *suffering* other – in other words, with someone who is (or who we believe to be) worse off than we are – is a particular kind of cultural imperative. From the mid eighteenth century, she argues,

[A] sense of self, of place in the world and identity, has frequently been articulated through the use of *someone else's* story of suffering, loss, exploitation, pain . . . Numerous guidebooks, from the philosophical tract to the sentimental novel, showed how the story of suffering, told by another, could be accessed and its pathos used for the art of self-construction. It was . . . absolutely necessary that the one who tells of suffering is a subordinate, an inferior (usually a social inferior): a *victim* of some kind. (Steedman, 1996: 107, emphasis in original)

Steedman's analysis might go some way towards explaining a current fascination with 'trauma narratives' or what has come to be known as 'mis lit' (misery literature). Memoirs detailing abusive childhoods, for example, appear to be enjoying (if that is the right word) an interest that shows no signs of fading. In March 2005, four of *The Bookseller*'s top ten hardback non-fiction titles and three of the top ten non-fiction paperbacks were memoirs of domestic abuse (Byrne, 2005). Perhaps these stories are compelling because they offer what Steedman argues we have come to see as an essential means for producing an identity – they offer narratives of suffering, in which the heroes are, in Lauren Berlant's words, 'the subject[s] of pain'.

Berlant (2000) writes of an increasing mobilizing of pain as a means of claiming authority. In what Gross and Hoffman (2004) have described as a contemporary 'victim culture', to be the subject of pain is almost to guarantee authority. That is, pain is understood as producing not only clarity but truth (Berlant, 2000). Berlant's argument is based on the United States, where 'the pursuit of happiness' is a constitutional right; and in this setting, she argues, injustice is understood as being guaranteed by feeling bad: conversely, feeling good is taken as 'evidence of justice's triumph' (Berlant, 2000: 35). I think, however, that, like Steedman's, her argument has a broader application.

In a similar vein to Steedman, Berlant suggests that those who are socially privileged often deal with their privilege through an identification with the trauma of the dominated and the dispossessed . But of course this identification can only be imaginary: those who are socially privileged are, by definition, *not* sharing in the misery of lacking privilege. Further, such suffering tends to be glamorized by an emphasis on 'trauma' (as opposed to misery, adversity or ordinary unhappiness). 'Trauma' suggests something extraordinary: as Berlant notes, trauma takes you out of your life, while ordinary, mundane adversity keeps you firmly within it.

If the quest for a specific type of identity leads to a move in which the narrative of the 'suffering other' is appropriated, this appropriation of the pain of others gives rise to troubles of its own. For one thing, it can obliterate the original suffering, making it (at worst) little more than a fashion accessory. Where, then, does this leave the person who originally produced the pain-full narrative (the one that is appropriated)? Bell hooks' impassioned and angry words on the subject of white people appropriating the pain narratives of people of colour is salutary:

> No need to heed your voice when I can talk about you better than you can speak about yourself. No need to hear your voice. Only tell me about your pain. I want to know your story. And then I will tell it back to you in a new way. Tell it back to you in such a way that it has become my own. Re-writing you I write myself anew. I am still author, authority. I am still colonizer, the speaking subject, and you are now at the center of my talk. (hooks, 1990: 151)

This is hooks speaking back, an example of the 'suffering other' who is marked as socially inferior, refusing silently to allow the appropriation of their narrative. This passage also shows the ways in which such an identification with the pain of others can be seen as unsettling the ethical stance outlined by Ricoeur. Ricoeur argues that the empathetic understanding produced through narrative – in which we put ourselves in the place of another, in another's story – is an important means of ethical identification. Richard Kearney glosses this stance as follows:

> Ricoeur praises narrative understanding – where one represents oneself as another – to the extent that it serves to liberate us from narcissistic interests without liquidating our identity. In so doing, it generates a basic act of empathy whereby the self flows from itself toward the other in a free variation of imagination . . . It transfigures the self-regarding self into a self-for-another. (Kearney, 2004: 174)

In other words, we behave ethically because we can imagine ourselves in others' stories. The 'subject of pain', then, might be seen as a distorted example of 'oneself as another'. In this case, instead of empathy, there is an *appropriation* of the pain of others. This is particularly acute at a time when pain is a powerful medium through which we get our stories heard, when pain is a medium for sociality. Pain, in other words, has become a powerful way through which we establish shared social ties. Further, pain has become a guarantee of authenticity. Not all pain is equally available as a resource in this way, however. As Steedman points out, the 'other' with whom we are supposed to identify should be a victim – that is, they must not be blameworthy in any way. Those who are understood as 'bringing misfortune on themselves' do not tend to become figures of identification.

To illustrate the point here, I shall briefly discuss one case where such identifications seem to have been very publicly made: that is, in a 'trauma memoir' which itself turned out to be fraudulent. This is the case of Binjamin Wilkomirski/Bruno Grosjean, which raises numerous issues not only about pain and identification but about memory, truth and falsehood. I want to point to some issues about a contemporary climate in which pain becomes a guarantee of authenticity and in which identifications are invited on this basis.

Very briefly, the 'facts' (as far as they are known) about this case are as follows. In 1995 Binjamin Wilkomirski's memoir, *Bruchstücke. Aus einer Kindheit 1939–1948*, was published in Germany. Several translations quickly followed, including the English version, *Fragments: Memories of a Childhood, 1939–1948*. The book, a memoir of a Jewish child's experiences in a Latvian ghetto and in Nazi death camps, received tremendous critical acclaim and numerous awards.[4]

Wilkomirski's account was unusual among Holocaust survivor memoirs in two ways: it was written to a high literary standard (it has been compared to the memoirs of Primo Levi and Elie Wiesel), and it told the story from the perspective of a child. The book was extremely well received. However, the plaudits heaped on Wilkomirski proved to be short-lived. Investigative work by a Swiss journalist, Daniel Ganzfried, and later by the Swiss historian, Stefan Maechler, revealed *Fragments* to be a false memoir. All available evidence indicated that 'Binjamin Wilkomirski' was born Bruno Grosjean, a Swiss Gentile, born to a single mother and subsequently adopted by a wealthy Swiss couple. He was neither Jewish nor Latvian, and had never been in a camp. Wilkomirski/Grosjean, however, refuses to acknowledge that the memoir is in any way fraudulent, and indeed has suggested that he considers an unwillingness to believe his story a form of Holocaust denial.

I do not want to attempt to offer any psychological reading of Wilkomirski here; I do not want to try to guess his motivations or indeed his 'real identity'. I am concerned, rather, with broader questions about what this case can tell us about the social production of narrative identity. It seems clear that extremely complex negotiations between self and other have taken place in his own life history. It is clear, for example, that Wilkomirski's 'real' early life was troubled and that this caused him pain. It is also clear that he had read numerous memoirs written by survivors of concentration camps and it seems that he had introduced certain elements of these accounts into his own story. In this, it might be suggested, Wilkomirski was simply doing what we all do in constituting our life narratives and indeed our narrative identities. However, the falsity of the memoir raises interesting issues about the relationship between identity, history, authority, politics and truth in a particular time and place (post-war Europe). To pursue this, I will briefly outline Gross and Hoffman's (2004) reading of the case, since it highlights so many of these points.

Gross and Hoffman suggest that Wilkomirski's identification with the Holocaust – even to the degree of inserting himself into a story that was not his – is perfectly coherent in a contemporary 'victim culture'. They write,

---

[4] I have taken this account of Wilkomirski's life largely from Maechler (2001). See also Eskin (2002).

It is easy to dismiss Wilkomirski as someone whose personal suffering has led him to over-identify with victims of the Holocaust, but in [a contemporary] victim culture . . . this is just what he is supposed to do. Institutions as influential as the US Holocaust Memorial Museum teach the Holocaust through transference and identification. (Gross and Hoffman, 2004: 34)

In other words, Wilkomirski has successfully achieved identification with 'the subject of pain', and it is hardly surprising that he has done so, especially 'In an age of identity politics, when being a victim is a mark of distinction' (Gross and Hoffman, 2004: 32). As an example of what they mean, Gross and Hoffman point to the Holocaust Memorial Museum in Washington DC, which assigns visitors identity cards with the names of victims on them. Visitors do not know at this point whether or not they will 'survive'. In this way, as they point out,

The emphasis is on the visceral, the emotive and the artifactual: the museum personalizes history, encouraging visitors to identify with and put themselves in the place of the victims. This is precisely what Wilkomirski has done. (Gross and Hoffman, 2004: 34)

Wilkomirski, then, has achieved a narrative identity, and analysts' accounts point to the likelihood that he himself is invested in this identity and in some sense believes it to be his own. But it is a narrative identity cast adrift from the facts of the case as embodied in official documents, and in the memories and life histories of others. Any one of these can be faulty, of course, but the weight of evidence would seem, on every count, to bear against the Wilkomirski story.

What can this false memoir tell us about narrative identity? It raises several issues, including the importance attached to the facticity (or otherwise) of accounts, the authority of the storyteller and the significance of the narratives and the memories of others. Wilkomirski used publicly circulating narratives to produce his own; from a narrative perspective, as I have suggested, this is what we all do. We use the available symbols to interpret and tell an identity and in the process we constitute our identities. So it is not this that marks out Wilkomirski's narrative. Rather, it is its distance from the publicly *agreed* narratives of historical facts. Does this matter? On the one hand, we might argue that it does not: that although the story does not correspond to historical facts, it speaks a different kind of 'truth' about its author. As Donna Haraway argues,

Stories are not 'fictions' in the sense of being 'made up'. Rather, narratives are devices to produce certain kinds of meaning. I try to use stories to tell what I think is the truth – a located, embodied, contingent and *therefore* real truth. (Haraway, 1997: 230, emphasis added)

Haraway seems to be suggesting that 'truth' is to be found in location, embodiment, contingency. I think that what lies behind this comment is Haraway's refusal to claim authority for her stories – a refusal to claim that any one account is the 'god's eye view' (Haraway, 1991). This is part of her critique of a spurious objectivity that claims to be able to see the world 'as it is', while really being the subjective position of those with the power to claim objectivity. In terms of Haraway's analysis of knowledge production, this has been an important critique. But to see 'truth' as inhering in locatedness leads us into difficulties when considering narratives like that contained in *Fragments*. Don't narratives make some moral claim for recognition?

According to Richard Kearney (2002), there is no moral obligation on fictional narratives to have any relationship to real events, but we do expect factual narratives to do so, and indeed the writers or tellers of narratives which are, or which purport to be, factual, themselves often demand that we read them in this way. If, on an aesthetic level, there is no need to determine whether the narrative corresponds to the facts, then it does matter at an ethical level.

From this perspective, and even though narrative, embedded in a hermeneutic tradition, is more concerned with interpretation and meaning than with positivistic 'facts', there is generally assumed to be some correspondence (however mediated and attenuated) between 'fact' and 'interpretation'. From the perspective of a narrative approach, it is the case neither that 'only the facts matter', nor that 'the facts don't matter at all' (and what matters is meaning). Rather, we might see fact and meaning as dialectically linked. There is no unmediated access to the 'facts of the matter'; we remember, we interpret those memories, we re-remember and reinterpret, and so on.

But this is not the same as dispensing with the facts altogether. Wilkomirski's story acquires a kind of authority associated with its pain and with its being about an obscene and shameful period in twentieth-century European history. We might say that he produced a fictional identity through assembling a fictional narrative out of a series of factual narratives. In the process, he might be seen to have become a different person – the 'subject of pain'. Stefan Maechler writes,

[Wilkomirski] truly blossomed in his role as concentration-camp victim, for it was in it that he finally found himself. There is every indication that Wilkomirski found his own narrative true and authentic because it unleashed such stunned silence, such waves of sympathy. Perhaps he did not really believe his story, but he did believe his own telling of it. Anything that had such an effect on listeners must be true. The glow in their eyes lent him a living, coherent identity – that of the greatest of all victims – and gave his story overwhelming authenticity. Without an audience, there would be no Wilkomirski. (Maechler, 2001: 273)

Audiences, however, tend to expect claims which are passed off as true (as in written memoirs or even spoken accounts) to accord with the 'facts'. Otherwise, some breach of sociality is seen to have occurred; the perpetrator of the lie has broken a set of social rules. This breach of a social contract or a social promise is key. Life narratives must accord *in some way*, not only with sets of intelligibility rules but with the accounts and memories and recordings of others. When they do not, a sense of betrayal frequently occurs. This is because, as I noted above, life narratives can never be individualized, atomized accounts, but must include some account of the lives of others. The ethical imperative seems to lie in a demand that narratives ought to be rendered sufficiently faithfully that others can recognize the story and, if they are sufficiently close to the storyteller, should be able to recognize themselves within it. This must go beyond an emotional identification ('yes, it was like that for me') to a more 'objective' identification ('yes, it was like that').

Of course there are numerous difficulties here since memory, as I noted above, is notoriously unreliable, and it is clearly the case that different people often remember the same event entirely differently – the source of many familial disputes. In many cases there are quite high degrees of tolerance over differences of interpretation. Moreover, even an overtly falsified narrative can be seen as acceptable in some circumstances (such as circumstances of extreme danger). Wilkomirski's narrative, however, was not only false but could not be attributed to an idiosyncrasy of interpretation – after all, he was either in the camps or he was not. But, crucially, his story laid claim to a 'privileged' suffering identity – that of Holocaust survivor. It may be, as Gross and Hoffman argue, that he was only obeying the demands of a culture that encourages identification with a suffering other – and indeed encourages the forging of an identity on that basis. But the public *response* to his life narrative would suggest that, however strong the tendency to value pain as a means of identification, this is not considered to be sufficient to guarantee the truth of an account. It would suggest, further, that some form of social contract is seen to be broken when people overtly fabricate an identity that does not accord with the narratives and lives of others (although, again, I must add, there are certain levels of tolerance in some circumstances, and not in others). It may be that *too closely* approximating the identity of 'victim' is seen as a breach of social rules, whereas the *appropriation of the suffering* of victims is increasingly acceptable.

The main point I want to make here is that the breach of sociality that is seen to occur when people take on a fraudulent identity is another indication of the inherently social character of narrative identity. Not only must identity-narratives conform to the specific 'intelligibility rules' of the time and place in which they are embedded, but they are also collective in the sense that no narrative identity belongs to the teller alone; they also incorporate the narratives of others. They must, as Hacking puts it, 'mesh with the rest of the world and with other people's stories, at least in externals' (Hacking, 1995: 251). As such, they must contribute to a form of sociality in which (within certain limits) they are seen as more or less according with the knowledge and experience and indeed the narratives of others.

The Wilkomirski case raises some troubling issues. It illustrates the ways in which people draw on a repertoire of existing narratives to produce their own narrative, the significance of an audience in receiving, understanding and interpreting a narrative, and the central importance of the time and space in which personal narratives are embedded. Wilkomirski produced a narrative identity but all the evidence indicates that he was not where he claimed to be; he did not live the life he claims as his own. In important ways, this makes his narrative false. If, however, he feels and experiences his identity as real (and I have no way of knowing whether or not he does), is it then real?

We might tentatively conclude that it is real to him, but that this is not enough. If this is so, then it tells us something important about the collective, deeply social character of any claimed identity. The contract between ourselves and others demands some minimal level of agreement, so that people cannot simply claim to be whatever and whoever they want, or, at least, such a move will not work without the consent and agreement of others. It is telling that Wilkomirski's narrative has come to be framed only in terms of what he is not: not Jewish, not Latvian, not a survivor of the camps. What he 'is' is absent, in the absence of an agreed, collective narrative. Without others, we are nothing.

Concluding remarks

In this chapter I have presented the view that identities are constituted through the stories we tell (to ourselves and to others) about them.

This perspective has to be seen in the context of a hermeneutic tradition that stresses the interpreted character of the social world. From this perspective, then, identity is produced through the interpretations people make out of the bits and pieces of their lives – interpretations that are put together to form an overall 'plot'.

Narratives and narrative identities plunge us into a sociality. They highlight the ways in which lives and identities are embedded in relationships. As such, they challenge the idea of the atomized individual. We remember and interpret according to social rules and social conventions; 'individual' narratives always incorporate others within them; and our narratives must, to some degree, accord with the narratives of others. It seems clear from the cautionary tale of the Wilkomirski case that, when they do not so accord, there is seen to be a breach of fundamental social rules. There are, then, limits on the ways in which we can 'borrow' from other stories, although borrow from these stories we must, since they are the interpretive resources available to us.

3 Who do you think you are? Kinship, inheritance and identity

Introduction

At the time of writing, BBC television is screening a weekly series in which 'celebrities' trace their ancestry. It is a curiously moving and intriguing series, and its title – 'Who do you think you are?' – is telling. Clearly, part of who the featured person is (and by extension, part of who all of 'us' are) is considered to lie in their forebears. In this programme and more generally in European and North American culture, inheritance is held to lead to identity. In this way, kinship is bound up with issues of identity, although not in any straightforward way. In answer to the (implicit) question, 'What are we?', this programme gives an answer in the form, 'We are the outcome of inherited material'.

The programme both derives from, and contributes to, a growing trend towards genealogical investigation in the form of tracing family trees, assisted by websites such as Genes Reunited. The programme's own website contains resources for this kind of investigation. What this trend indicates, I would suggest, is a concern with constituting identities within the context of a kin structure.

In one way, this of course is of a piece with current trends towards genetic determinism, discussed later in the chapter. In this form of determinism, identities are understood in terms of what is genetically inherited. Yet to cast the programme wholly in these terms would be misleading. Simply gaining genetic information (such as hair and eye colour, height etc.) would not exactly make it compelling viewing: rather, ancestors are, in a sense, 'brought to life', made real through description that is more than physical or physiological. Links are traced between the person 'fronting' the programme and her or his precursors. The person who is the focus of the programme makes sense of their own identity through invoking ancestral character traits: very often, they speak of their pride at the achievements or the strength of character of their forebears. What is stressed, then, are forms of individual identity embedded within a collective (familial, kin) identity.

This form of identity-constitution raises important questions about individualism and collectivism, about the place of various forms of inheritance, and about the shifting relations between 'nature' and 'culture'. Ultimately, it exposes some of the contradictory ways in which identity is understood and 'done' in the contemporary West. Further, kinship points up a number of contradictions in understandings of the person – for example, between the individual and the collective, the natural and the social – and has important ramifications for thinking about identity, both within and beyond kinship.

In referring to 'kinship' here, I am referring not simply to the doing of familial relationships – although that 'doing' is an important way in which we embed ourselves and others within a kin system (Morgan, 1996) – but to a whole network of ties which may or may not be characterized as 'blood ties', which typically involve various conceptualizations of relationships and which may (though they may not) involve various obligations. As we shall see, questions of definition are by no means straightforward in this area, but it is worth at this point noting Janet Carsten's comment that 'Conceived in its broadest sense, relatedness (or kinship) is simply about the ways in which people create similarity or difference between themselves and others' (Carsten, 2004: 82). Kinship, then, is a way of constituting relationships that include some and exclude others. It is, further, a way of constituting oneself within networks of relationships. As Sarah Franklin argues, 'Establishing identities is kinship work in action' (Franklin, 2000: 221). As I shall discuss in the following sections, kinship matters, but *how* it matters is by no means straightforward.

The archaic family?

It might immediately be objected that a concern with tracing one's family tree is an issue very different from the 'doing' of family relationships. Indeed, this is the case, and one does not necessarily imply the other (Binks, 2006). As I discuss further below, however, both genealogical tracing and the doing of family – together with an understanding of oneself in terms of kinship – are interrelated. 'But', a critic might further object, 'the family is in decline, and what's more, individualism is the prevailing idiom of personhood. Familial ties are just not so important.'

I would not want to deny the important social, political, cultural and economic changes that have occurred to *change* many aspects of the family, but the suggestion that families are in a sort of terminal decline goes against the evidence. To be sure, divorce rates, and rates of single parenthood, are rising across many European countries, and in the United States. On the other hand, there is relative stability.[1] Couple relationships – whether same- or other-sex – seem to be going strong. Single-parenthood is typically a temporary state and most people marry. Reports of the decline of 'the family' may simply be expressing a decline in stable, 'for life' heterosexual marriage and the nuclear family (Smart and Neale, 1999). But the decline in such forms does not signify the 'end of the family'. Indeed, much of the rhetoric about the 'decline' or 'end' of the family rests on mythic origins, on, for example, an appeal to 'traditional' family forms in which kinship ties were close and extended, or (a different kind of tradition) to an idealized nuclear (i.e. non-extended) family, in which gender roles were straightforward, children were better cared for and so on. There is much reason to distrust such mythical 'histories'; as Deborah Chambers wryly notes, for example, narratives in which families in the pre-industrial era are assumed to be characterized by extended, close-knit kin ties and in which this family type became gradually transformed into the modern nuclear family represents a set of myths that 'is vague in its periodisation, claiming, rather suspiciously, that the modern family emerged just before living memory' (Chambers, 2001: 36). What is clear is that there is a *diversification* of family forms as people increasingly live in 'reconstituted' families (Finch and Mason, 2000) or, indeed, in 'families of choice' (Weston, 1991). It is

---

[1] For example, in the United Kingdom the number of divorces peaked in 1993 at 180,018. In 2004, the figure had gone down to 167,116, a 0.2 per cent rise on the previous year. The number of marriages rose in 2004, for the third year running (311,180). About 60 per cent of women and men in the UK live as heterosexual couples. Of these, 90 per cent are married. There was a doubling of the proportion of households headed by a single parent between the early 1970s and 2002 – but only from 3 per cent to 6 per cent (Office for National Statistics (ONS), online at http://www.statistics.gov.uk/). At the point at which the Civil Partnership Act came into force in December 2005 (allowing same-sex couples rights similar to marital rights), more than 1,200 partnership ceremonies were scheduled across the United Kingdom. By August 2006 more than 6,500 couples had opted for civil partnerships (Muir, 2006).

not, then, that 'the family' has declined; rather, its form is changing (and has always changed).

If familial relationships remain significant, it is important to ask – especially in the context of discussions of identity – what family and kinship *mean* to people. Here again, there is a powerful theoretical and political trend which emphasizes the individualism of the contemporary social world in ways that suggest that kinship is not a reference point in people's lives or in their sense of themselves. This trend finds theoretical expression in the 'reflexive individualization thesis'. There are various versions of this thesis, but, in broad terms, its proponents argue that we are witnessing a disembedding (of old ways of life) and re-embedding (of new ones) in industrial society 'in which individuals must produce, stage and cobble together their biographies themselves' (Beck, 1994: 13). Identity here becomes a bricolage (Lash, 1994), something put together by the person in a series of creative acts. The comparison here is with a past in which ascriptive ties and traditional forms of authority held sway. By implication, such ties and such forms of authority no longer have a hold – or, at least, no longer have the hold they once did. Whether directly or indirectly, reflexive individualization theorists suggest that kin ties have a weakened place in the production of identities. The emphasis on an allegedly plastic, adaptive self, suited to global networks, suggests that the self is no longer produced through the (relatively) local networks of family and kin.

Nor is this emphasis confined to social theory: much of the political rhetoric of successive UK governments has centred on the notion of an endlessly self-fashioning individual. Kinship is invoked primarily in relation to poor whites, in relation to whom 'The biological metaphors of breeding and generation are key' (Haylett, 2001: 363) in concepts such as 'cycles of deprivation' and 'generations of disadvantage'. Such concepts characterize kin ties as almost atavistic. Frequently, they are implicitly represented as ties that bind us unhealthily to a past in which ascriptive categories – especially those of race, class and gender – threaten to swamp our 'individuality'.

The reflexive individualization thesis relies on the premise that categories such as class, race and gender *really are* less (rather than simply differently) important now than they were in the recent past. This premise has been strenuously challenged by a number of commentators, who have detailed the numerous and multifaceted ways in which these categories continue to matter. Further, several writers have shown the many ways in which people do *not* act on the basis of following a goal of personal fulfilment, but engage in what has been called a 'reflexive relationalism' (Finch and Mason, 2000), considering themselves and their lives in the context of networks of relationships, many of them kin relationships.

On the other hand, it is clear that there is a sort of theoretical or rhetorical commitment to individualism in the West, such that there is, in many spheres of life, a normative individualism, a suggestion that not only *are* we autonomous individuals, but this is as things *ought to be*. If, however, there is evidence that people do not necessarily live like this or understand themselves in this way – or at least do not always do so – then we seem to be in the middle of a tension here between competing understandings of identity and personhood. One problem, in terms of analysis, may be that like is not being compared with like, so that reflexive individualization theorists are relying on 'public' expressions of personhood rather than on what people actually do 'on the ground' – which may be rather different. As Carsten notes, in a somewhat different, though related, context,

> While fully acknowledging the importance of the value of individualism in the West, and its prominent expression in many legal, medical, philosophical, and religious discourses, it is important to recognize that Western notions of the person express other values too. These are present in very familiar and everyday contexts, and they also evoke qualities similar to those that anthropologists have been accustomed to attribute to persons in non-Western cultures. (Carsten, 2004: 97)

However, this is about more than the difference between 'public' discourses and 'private' lives: it is also about the ability of social actors to hold competing and contradictory views of the person. An emphasis *only* on individualism or individualization obscures the fact that people seem to be quite capable of holding contradictory views about the person simultaneously. This suggests that social actors are more capable of managing different, and even competing, models of personhood than many social theorists allow (Moore, 1994; Lawler, 2000). Carsten goes on to argue that being 'oneself' and being a relation are 'quite intertwined', and suggests that Westerners are perfectly well accustomed to seeing themselves and others in this way. I return to this issue below, but at this point I want to suggest that *kinship itself* might represent a way through the apparent contradiction between individualism and the collective ties of kin identities for Western persons. Michael Erben, for example, in his discussion of genealogy, argues that, 'In searching for and finding ancestors one is establishing both communality and individuality (sameness and differences)' (Erben, 1991: 276), adding,

> The more one journeys back the more one has in common with others, but there is too the realisation that an enormous number of historical persons have resulted in a single, unique, current individual . . . Perhaps genealogy is an area of human endeavour in which the practitioner can experience simultaneously connectedness and separation. (Erben, 1991: 277)

If genealogy provides both connectedness and separation, this, I would argue, is because Westerners understand both as necessary elements of kinship itself. Kinship connects us to wider networks and embeds us in them, yet it is through kinship that we are produced as unique individuals. I return to this below; the next section gives some background to the study of kinship and discusses how understandings of kinship and identity are organized within Western cultures.

Kinship (and) identity

Conventionally, the study of kinship has been the domain of anthropology rather than sociology, and this, in large part, stemmed from an assumption that while non-Westerners (the objects of study in traditional anthropology) had kinship, 'we' (in the West) have 'families' (see Carsten, 2004). The distinction is more than semantic. Although there have been different traditions in the analysis of kinship within 'traditional' social anthropology, what was common was a view of kinship as absolutely central and foundational to the social and cultural organization of non-Western societies. Kinship was the basic conceptual grid on to which all relationships could be mapped. Further, it was understood as a means – if not *the* means – through which non-Western identities were forged. Non-Westerners, in other words, have long been seen as having an identity based on and in kinship ties. In contrast, while the nuclear family was taken to be a central 'building block' of society within classical sociology, it was typically understood as one institution among many, rather than as the central foundation of culture. Western identities have not tended to be seen within the matrix of inherited kin material: indeed, Westerners have been attributed an agency that is almost certainly overstated in that they have been seen to be making *themselves*.

Recent developments – theoretical, social and political – have underscored the inadequacy of such a model. It is clearly inadequate to see 'the family' as a discrete realm, separated from other social forms, not least because the meanings around what constitutes 'a family' inform wider debates and decisions on the regulation of sexuality, rules of inheritance, the placing or creation of children and so on (see Haimes, 2003). Families are important means of transmitting material and cultural privilege: stories of their demise notwithstanding, they occupy a central place in Western social life. As Finch and Mason argue, 'family relationships lie at the heart of understanding the condition of social life in advanced industrial, or late modern, societies' (Finch and Mason, 2000: 5). And, I would add, they are at the heart of understandings of identity, both through the 'doing' of family relationships, and through understandings of kin groups and one's place within them.

Sociologists of the family have long studied people's sense of place within kin systems and the place of the family within wider social and cultural arrangements (for an overview, see Allen, 1999). Anthropologists have increasingly turned their analytic attention to Western societies and in the process have shown how kinship is an important organizing principle of such societies and that it remains central to how Western persons understand themselves *as* persons.

A pivotal text in the process of turning an anthropological gaze on Western kin systems was David Schneider's *American Kinship,* first published in 1968. In this work, Schneider shifted the focus of kinship studies from the *function* of kinship (the ways in which kinship organizes culture) to its *meaning* – what kinship *means* to social actors. As the title implies, Schneider's specific focus was on America – or more precisely, on the United States – but his work has broader relevance than this and has been influential (although not uncritically accepted) in subsequent studies of European, as well as of American, kinship.

Schneider's fundamental argument is that Americans conceptualize kinship as cohering around two orders – the order of blood and the order of law. In other words, when Americans think about kinship they consider networks of people who are related through 'blood' (children and parents, siblings, cousins, etc.) or through 'law' (spouses, in-laws). At first glance it may seem that 'blood' ties are ties based in 'nature' and 'law' ties are ties based in 'culture': in other words, the blood/law distinction can look like a reiteration of a nature/culture divide. This indeed may be the way in which social actors think of these ties (although, equally, it may not be). However, it is not how Schneider is using the distinction. His argument is that the distinction is *itself* cultural. Americans recognize certain kin as 'blood' relatives because they understand the self as biologically linked to others. Blood *symbolizes* connection: it is not itself connection. In other words, the meanings we give to blood (a metaphor for a 'natural' substance of some kind) enables Americans (and Europeans) to build cultural relations of kin. Kin relations are, *by definition*, cultural. Kin are quite simply those persons we *recognize* as kin. But we recognize them according to the two orders of blood and law.

Nevertheless, Schneider argues, in the everyday usage of kinship, 'blood' ties are understood as being especially significant. Unlike legal ties, they cannot ordinarily be dissolved, although a relative may be disowned and disavowed. No doubt this is linked with a cultural belief that the blood relationship is 'an objective fact of nature' (Schneider, 1968: 24). More fundamentally, 'blood' links are understood as central in terms of forging an identity. Schneider argues,

> A blood relationship is a relationship of identity. People who are blood rel-
> atives share a common identity, they believe. This is expressed as 'being
> of the same flesh and blood'. It is a belief in common biological constitu-
> tion, and aspects like temperament, build, physiognomy and habits are
> noted as signs of this shared biological makeup, this special identity of rel-
> atives with each other. Children are said to look like their parents, or to
> 'take after' one or another parent or grandparent; these are confirming
> signs of the common biological identity. A parent, particularly a mother,
> may speak of a child as 'a part of me'. (Schneider, 1968: 25)

This is certainly what I found in research I conducted on mother–daughter relationships in which mothers used expressions such as 'bits of her that are bits of me' when talking of their daughters. I have argued in discussing that research that in conceptualizing their daughters (and themselves) in this way, women were tying their own and their daughters' identities firmly within a kin system, in which characteristics could be explained through inheritance (Lawler, 2000). But it is important to note that Westerners do not see parents as simply *reproducing* themselves in their children. Strathern argues,

> The child's physical origins lie in the bodies of others, a link as indissolu-
> ble as its own genetic formation is normally deemed irreversible. Yet
> parents only reproduce parts of themselves. Like the fortune one may or
> may not be born into, the conjunction of genetic traits is assumed to be
> fortuitous. While the child claims its origins in its parents' make-up, it
> itself evinces a unique combination of characteristics, and the combi-
> nation is a matter of chance. This lays the basis of its individuality.
> Individuality is expected to assist the child to develop that independence
> which is one manifestation of it (hence the lesser expectation of duty). At
> the same time, 'individuals' must also be seen as making themselves.
> Although the basis for the link between parent and child lies in the child's

past, what that link means in the future is contingent on how the individual person acts. The nature of interaction, the degree of obligation felt . . . all depend on what the child will *make* of its past. (Strathern, 1992b: 166)

This brings us back to Erben's argument, discussed briefly above, that genealogy – and, by extension, 'doing' kinship more generally – is an important way in which Westerners constitute themselves *both* as tied within a kin system (a collectivity) *and* as unique, individual persons. It is the very collectivity of kinship that is understood as producing the individual. Of English kinship (though, again, the argument has a wider application) Strathern notes,

[T]he particular social relationship of parent and child generates the image of the child not just as a son or daughter but as a unique individual. Indeed, we might consider *the individuality of persons as the first fact of English kinship.* (Strathern, 1992a: 14, emphasis in original)

As Finch and Mason note, Strathern is not pointing here to English culture as made up of atomized individuals. Rather, 'the very idea of individualism comes *from* relationships and their social meaning and, in that sense, is produced *by* kinship' (Finch and Mason, 2000: 18, emphasis in original).

Drawing on Strathern's insights, I have argued elsewhere (Lawler, 2000) that *recognition* is a nodal point in determining what the child 'makes of its past'. It is recognition, I argued, that stands between absolute choice (being whatever you want) and absolute determinism (being the same as your forebears). The women in the *Mothering the Self* study only recognized *some* traits of *some* family members as contributing to their own (and their daughters') identities. Some traits could be disowned and others embraced. This is active identity-work in the context of kinship.

Strathern's analysis of the ways in which Westerners understand their identities as inherited while that inheritance leads to individuality is crucial in addressing what looks like a fundamental contradiction in Western kinship: that persons are seen as unique, bounded individuals *at the same time* that they are understood as being placed within systems of kin ties. We see an apparent contradiction between two models of the self: on the one hand, the self as an autonomous entity, ending at the skin, individual and unique, and, on the other, the self as the embodiment of relationships.

I shall explore this apparent contradiction further below. But at this point – and because the model of personhood outlined by Strathern is likely to seem normal and obvious to most Europeans and North

Americans – it is worth considering how persons might be thought of if they were *not* considered as unique, bounded individuals. In other words, what is the contrast with which Strathern is working? How else could we be persons?

Strathern's early research was in Melanesia and she usefully brings to her analysis the contrasting views of personhood and kinship used by Melanesians (Strathern, 1988, 1992b, 1996). Westerners, Strathern argues, see themselves as *individual* persons (that is, unable to be divided) to whom relationships are then added: a view that might be paraphrased as 'I am "myself" and I will then *have* relationships of various kinds, including kin relations. I might become social, but I am not inherently so.' Melanesians, however, see persons as the embodiment of relationships: persons are *inherently* social. It is not simply that they are the embodiment of various roles; rather, they have relationships built into them. This might be paraphrased as 'Who I am is the embodiment of the various relationships in which I have been and am embedded, including my place in the social world.' While Westerners typically see identity in terms of a core that endures across different contexts, Melanesians, Strathern suggests, see identity as inconceivable outside its context; they are dividual (able to be divided) as well as individual (unable to be divided), since their identities embody a sociality:

> Far from being regarded as unique entities, Melanesian persons are as dividually as they are individually conceived. They contain a generalized sociality within. Indeed, persons are frequently constructed as the plural and composite site of relationships that produced them. The singular person can be imagined as a social microcosm. (Strathern, 1988: 13)

To summarize so far: I have argued that kinship remains significant in doing various kinds of 'identity work'. Kinship, at the very least, is a system for determining to whom we are related: as such it must also specify identities as they exist within constellations of relatives. Perhaps this can be seen most clearly in particularly 'troubled' kin narratives, when kin or kin ties are seen to be in some way absent. The next section explores the notion of identity-through-kinship in the context of narratives of adoption, and of conception through donor insemination.

Identity crises? Stories of absent parents

In June 2002, Joanna Rose obtained a ruling in the High Court in the United Kingdom that she was entitled to have access to 'non-identifying information' about her sperm donor father (*Joanna Rose & E (a child)* v. *the Secretary of State for Health & the Human Fertilisation & Embryology Authority*). Invoking the Human Rights Act of 1998, the Court ruled that Rose was entitled to this information as a means of establishing her *identity*. This linking of the right to know one's identity with the right to know one's parentage is an interesting manifestation of the continuing significance of kinship even in the face of an emphasis on individualism that is particularly apparent in, although not exclusive to, 'troubled' narratives in which parentage is seen to be missing or broken.

Several studies of people who have been adopted stress the ways in which notions of identity are central to the search for birth parents. Janet Carsten, for example, when asking adoptees what had motivated them to seek out their birth parents, typically received the responses 'To find out who I am', or 'To be complete' (Carsten, 2004: 147). Eleanor Ott, an adoptee cited in Yngvesson and Mahoney's (2000) article, claims, '*A person who does not know her ancestry is denied access to who she really is*' (Eleanor Ott, in Yngvesson and Mahoney, 2000: 92, emphasis Yngvesson and Mahoney's).[2] This seems a common sentiment and appears to be especially expressed by those people who have been adopted under systems of 'closed' adoption (in which birth records are sealed). Indeed, this is one important reason why there is a great deal of lobbying, in countries which practise such systems, for birth records to be open. Adoptions in the United States and Canada are governed by state or provincial law, and the extent to which adoptees are entitled to see their birth records varies from state to state and from province to province. (Currently, only five states in the United States practise open adoption, in which adoptees (above the age of majority) are entitled to see their original birth certificate.) By contrast, in all the countries of the United Kingdom open adoption is practised and adoptees over the age of 18 are entitled to request information that will enable them to obtain a copy of their original birth certificate.

Certainly, where closed adoption is practised, there is evidence to indicate that people are left with a sense of 'identity crisis'. For example,

---

[2] The women cited in Yngvesson and Mahoney were giving evidence at the Vermont House Judiciary Committee on Health and Welfare, convened to discuss a draft proposal of a new adoption statute, during 1995 and 1996. The draft law 'expanded birth father rights and sought to open adoption records' (Yngvesson and Mahoney, 2000: 91).

> Everyone but adoptees can look in [to the family] and see themselves reflected. I didn't know what it was like to be me. I felt like someone who looks into a mirror and sees no reflection. I felt lonely, not connected to anything, floating, like a ghost. ('Rachel' in Lifton, 1994: 68)

> Even though I did not know I was not their child, I felt as though I was not – something did not fit in. It was as though I did not really belong to them, or to anyone, or anywhere. (Sheila Demeako, in Yngvesson and Mahoney, 2000: 93)

What is being expressed here is a deep sense of displacement. This seems to be related to a sense of *not knowing*, itself related to *not belonging*. As Yngvesson and Mahoney argue,

> Adoption stories reveal the dis-ease of being forced to a hard game of identity difference together in the context of powerful narratives that compel us to situate ourselves in one place or another. (Yngvesson and Mahoney, 2000: 78)

This 'situating of the self', they suggest, takes place, at least in part, through the development of a self-narrative that starts, not at one's own birth, but with one's forebears. This in turn points to the significance of a wider network, stretching back through time, as a resource in constituting identity. It might be thought that a hiatus in the life narrative (see chapter 2) experienced by adoptees gives rise to this sense of displacement: that there is a sense of having been one thing (a member of family A) which is then displaced by having to become a different thing (a member of family B). However, we find similar sentiments expressed by people who have been conceived through donor insemination (DI), who have not experienced such a hiatus.

DI is a rather low-tech procedure in which a woman's egg is fertilized using donated semen. When this is used by a woman in a heterosexual partnership, it is likely that the assumption will be that the father of the resulting child is her male partner – and indeed the encouragement of such assumptions, on the part of the resultant child(ren) and of others, has conventionally been encouraged by the medical profession. Hence there is no 'external' pressure for disclosure (as might be the case if an older child is adopted, for example). However, a relatively recent emphasis on openness and disclosure might indicate that it may be more likely that children conceived in this way are (at some point) told of their origins. Further, and as the case of Joanna Rose highlights, there is a legal impetus towards (limited) disclosure.

Turner and Coyle (2000) collected the accounts of sixteen people aged between 26 and 55, all of whom had been conceived through DI.

Their respondents were contacted through DI support groups in the United Kingdom, the United States, Canada and Australia. The interviewees had experienced a wide diversity in terms of how, when and where they found out about their conception. Nevertheless, what is common to many of their accounts is an emphasis on 'troubled' identity. In the following extracts, research participants are discussing how they felt when they found out about their conception (in all cases the emphasis is mine):

> Part of me was shaken and profoundly shocked. Part of me was utterly calm, as things *suddenly fell into place*, and I was faced with an immediate reappraisal of *my own identity*. ('Imogen', in Turner and Coyle, 2000: 2044)

> My initial reaction was to laugh. I thought it was hysterical. The man I thought was my dad was such a creep that it was nice to know I wasn't genetically related to him. I guess *it changed my view of my identity*. It changed it in a positive way. Instead of being the child of this terrible man [her social father], I was probably the daughter of a doctor [the donor]. ('Phoebe', in Turner and Coyle, 2000: 2045)

> I always felt like I didn't belong with these people [her parents]. ('Rachel', in Turner and Coyle, 2000: 2045)

> I needed to know whose face I was looking at in the mirror – I needed to know *who I was* and how I came to be. ('Rachel', in Turner and Coyle, 2000: 2046)

In Rachel's account here, we see identity being invoked through a (literal, visual) recognition of 'who she was', in this case, who she looked like. For Phoebe, Imogen and Rachel, the knowledge that their social fathers are not genetically related to them brings into train a new sense of their identity, as (in Imogen's case) things 'fell into place'. Imogen and (especially) Rachel narrate themselves through an expression of never fitting. Sometimes, in the narratives of both adoptees and DI children, this expression of 'never fitting' is narrated in terms of having a different appearance from that of siblings or other family members. But often it is expressed as a more diffuse and amorphous 'knowledge' about 'not fitting' – a knowledge that is sometimes linked to some kind of 'genetic knowledge'. But it is important to remember that the people conceived through DI *are* genetically related to their mothers. More significantly, perhaps, what they narrate here was also narrated by some of the women in my (2000) study of mothers and daughters by women who (to their knowledge at least) were genetically related to *both* their social parents. The women in my own study who expressed this kind of sentiment did, however, share one other thing – they occupied a different social class from their mothers. I suggested in *Mothering the Self* that these women were telling a story of themselves in which their birth mother was written out. What we find in many of Turner and Coyle's respondents is a desire to tell a story of the self in which the genetic father (the donor) is written in, and/or the social father is written out. So the location of self and others within a kin system is creative work. Further, for all of them, notions of inheritance are extremely important in their sense of 'who they are', and we can see in their accounts attempts to make identities on the basis of notions of what they inherit – whether or not that inheritance is 'real'.

There remains a powerful cultural narrative which constitutes identity in this way and it is therefore no surprise that people who have been adopted or born through DI may feel a sense of dislocation from such understandings. Adoption and DI bring 'trouble' to narratives through which, according to Paul Ricoeur, lives are understood and constituted as coherent (Ricoeur, 1991b; Somers and Gibson, 1994; Ewick and Silbey, 1995), through which identities are *made*.

Generally, in narratives generated by people who have been adopted or conceived through DI, there are many expressions of a sense of a loss of part of the self. This problem may take many forms, but is commonly expressed as having a missing or partial self, not knowing the true self, being unaware of who one 'really' is, or having a self that is out of place or does not belong where it is. Although in some cases this is represented in terms of a need for genetic information – for example, about medical conditions – it seems that simply the provision of a genomic map would not suffice. As Turner and Coyle argue in their study of donor offspring,

> [T]hese donor offspring perceived a sense of abandonment of responsibility by their donor fathers and the medical profession. They expressed a need and a right to know who their donor fathers are and, if possible, to have some sort of relationship with them. It seems that for these donor offspring 'non identifying' [i.e. genetic] information might not be sufficient to meet their needs. (Turner and Coyle, 2000: 2050)

A linking of identity with kinship – or at least with ancestry – is one that is enshrined in international law and informs public discourse. The notion of identity as deriving from an inheritance, itself derived from kin members, is institutionalized to the extent that it is found in various forms of legislation. For example, Article 8 of the UN

Convention on the Rights of the Child inscribes 'family relations' as a part of identity when it states that

> 1. Parties undertake to respect the right of the child to preserve his or her identity, including nationality, name and family relations as recognized by law, without unlawful interference.
> 2. Where a child is illegally deprived of some or all of the elements of his or her identity, States Parties shall provide appropriate assistance and protection, with a view to re-establishing speedily his or her identity.

Relevant European law is enshrined in Article 8 of the Human Rights Act (1998) (an act which incorporates the European Convention on Human Rights into English law and the Act used by Joanna Rose, discussed above). This law seems less explicitly about inherited identity, but has been used to argue for the right of those conceived through DI to receive non-identifying information about the donor on the basis that a 'right to family life' implies a 'right to an identity'. How could one not have an identity? The 'identity' being referenced here is the right to knowledge about one's forebears (in the test case, non-identifying knowledge of a genetic father – i.e. the sperm donor). (There is no equivalent in US state or federal law, although there are voluntary donor identity programmes in existence.) Article 8 states,

> 1. Everyone has the right to respect for his private and family life, his home and his correspondence.
> 2. There shall be no interference by a public authority with the exercise of this right except such as is in accordance with the law and is necessary in a democratic society in the interests of national security, public safety or the economic well-being of the country, for the prevention of disorder or crime, for the protection of health or morals, or for the protection of the rights and freedoms of others.

So what we see here are powerful cultural and legal discourses which embed identity in a kin system at the same time as unique and autonomous individuality is stressed. These kin ties are held to generate us rather than to fix us in place: indeed, there is a powerful cultural expectation that they *ought not* to fix us in place, that we ought not to be held in position by the tentacles of the past. This is held to be the case whether our parents are millionaires or paupers, although in practice of course, one's life chances are very different in the two circumstances. Nevertheless, kin ties remain significant within these discourses.

In accounts of people conceived through DI and adoptees, there is an active making of an identity, based on including or denying real or imagined kin. It is a very clear example of kinship as something that is *done*; and as something out of which an identity is *actively formed*. There are difficulties here, as an authentic, stable identity based on kinship seems constantly to slip away and evade one's grasp. Is this because of these people's unusual circumstances, or are they simply more aware of, and therefore, highlighting, a more generalized search for a stable identity that must ultimately fail? For Yngvesson and Mahoney, it is the latter:

> The experience of adoptees only serves to throw into relief what is surely a common, though sometimes, subtle, experience of the arbitrariness of belonging and of the identities (individual, collective) that are constructed across this fragile scaffolding [of a 'bloodline']. (Yngvesson and Mahoney, 2000: 102)

By way of illustration, they cite the example of Yngvesson's own sister-in-law – dark haired in a family of fair-haired people – who, growing up in rural Sweden, was frequently asked 'where she came from'. They continue, 'The very desire for an authentic identity inevitably results in its being challenged because no-one can live it, it places everyone "outside" belonging' (Yngvesson and Mahoney, 2000: 104).

So, for Yngvesson and Mahoney, no one can *really* have the authentic, connected kinship identity of fantasy, but it is in these stories that we see the difficulties most clearly. If identity is a central concern in these cases, this is not because kinship identity is important only to these 'non-conventional' cases, but because these cases highlight the important but taken-for-granted character of inherited identity more generally. In its (perceived) absence, we see the significance of kin relationships in forming and embedding identities.

Although, as I have indicated, it seems that the search for identity-through-kin is about much more than a desire for genetic knowledge, the language of genetic relatedness is often invoked, as phenomena such as appearance and temperament are invoked. Moreover, the language of genetic relatedness currently enjoys a particular prominence for Westerners. The next section explores some of the issues involved, particularly for considerations of 'nature' and 'culture.

Genes are us? Nature, culture and inheritance

As we saw above, the notion of 'natural' relatedness through genetic ties is an important way in which Western persons typically configure kinship. But it is considered that such ties have to be made into something. More generally, a concern with the *relationship* between 'nature' and 'culture' seems to be motivating contemporary 'troubles', from the use of reproductive technologies to cloning and global warming. And kinship stands, in many cases, as something which is seen to embody this relationship. As I suggested earlier, in kinship we do cultural work in making ties in which we *recognize* certain persons as kin. But this recognition is often – although not always and not necessarily – held to work on the basis of some 'natural' substance.

One way in which kinship especially resonates in the contemporary climate is through the concept of inherited DNA. Donna Haraway (1997) traces the development in understandings of kinship and the human person and argues that we have moved from the metaphor of 'blood' to that of 'genes' as being both what we inherit and what makes us who we are. Paul Rabinow (1996) argues that, because of recent genetic-technological developments and the prominence of genetic research (including the Genome Project), contemporary Westerners now use DNA as a *synecdoche*. A synecdoche is a figure of speech in which parts come to stand for the whole (as in 'wheels' to mean 'car'). What is being suggested here is that genes have come to stand for who we are: this is summed up in the notion that we *are* our genetic material.

At a genetic or biological level, this is clearly inadequate – if we are no more than our genes then not only clones but also identical twins must be the same person. While cloning has given rise to considerable public anxiety about the nature of the person, most cultures have managed to live with the idea of identical twins for a long time. Nevertheless, the idea of 'natural ties' and 'natural material' – expressed by Schneider in the metaphor of blood but increasingly using the metaphor of 'genes' – remains a powerful cultural formulation for thinking about inherited identity. Often, when 'natural' ties are invoked, they are understood as inhering in genetic material.

This matters on several registers. Those who would claim that our identity is a product of our 'biology' or 'genetics' are often also invoking a human 'nature'. We need to pause here to think about what is being invoked when 'nature' is being invoked. There are various ways in which 'nature' is used: as something to be overcome, for example (as in ideas of cultivation – whether of land or of people). It is also used as something which is desirable (when it is opposed to 'artifice'). But a further very powerful way in which nature is used is to signify something which cannot be altered. Nature tends to be what is 'given', and opposed to culture which is understood as being 'made' (Carsten, 2004). This usage pits 'nature' against 'culture' with culture being understood as produced by humans; and if produced, therefore capable of being remade in different forms – as more or less endlessly malleable. Against this, 'nature' is understood as only marginally susceptible to human intervention (as in predictions about global warming, for example). While it may change, it is held to be resistant to human intervention. So when, for example, 'nature' is invoked to explain differences between male and female identities, the implication is that such identities *cannot be* or *ought not to be* changed. An immensely powerful legitimating mechanism is at work.

But we push up against some interesting developments with this usage. First, it would be mistaken to think of 'culture' as being endlessly malleable. It is clear that cultures change, but this does not mean that they are easily changeable. They are embedded in practices and relations, they come to seem obvious (and even 'natural') and people become attached to them, so that change may be difficult to effect even at an individual level. One example of the apparent fixity of culture is that of language. Leaving aside questions of 'deep grammar' (Chomsky, 1986), it is clear that the development of *specific* languages is socially constructed, and that a facility with any language only comes about because we have learned that language. Languages, then, are social. Yet we cannot suddenly 'know' another language, and most people have the greatest facility in their so-called 'mother tongue'. Still less can we decide to overturn the rules of language by deciding to put words in any order at all. In such a world, communication would be impossible. But if language is difficult to change, this is not because specific languages are somehow 'natural': they are not.

Conversely, (what we refer to as) 'nature' itself is far from being unchanging or unchangeable. Humans intervene in 'nature' all the time, usually without an anxiety that nature is being 'undone'. Recent developments might be seen as accelerating this trend. From the start, genetic research has been concerned, not simply with describing or explaining, but with *changing*, and with changing things which are often conceptualized as unchangeable (such as genes). This is a new form of determinism, but, Sarah Franklin (2000) argues, it is a determinism that is oddly flexible in many of its manifestations. 'Life itself' becomes information – as in, for example, the map of the human genome. But, Franklin argues, it is *reprogrammable* information.

So it would be mistaken to see 'nature' (embodied in 'genes' or 'blood') as unchanging and unchangeable, and 'culture' as easily and effortlessly malleable. Perhaps instead it would be more productive to see 'nature' *as a concept* used by Westerners to designate what is 'given' (before, or outside, human intervention), and 'culture' as the term they/we give to what seems evidently to be made through human effort. Formulated in this way, it is possible to confound rather sterile debates about what *really* belongs to 'nature' and what to 'nurture' in identities, and to put the emphasis on how people themselves consider, understand and do identity in the context of kinship. This formulation also allows us to reconsider conventional understandings of 'natural' ties as inhering in bodily substances (blood, genes, DNA), while 'cultural' ties inhere in effort (the work of care, commitment), and it also allows us to bypass the conventional divide between 'the biological' and 'the social'.

Certainly, and as Carsten (2004) points out, an opposition between 'nature' and culture' has held sway in the West for at least two hundred years, but while it may have been a powerful public expression of ordering the world, it does not follow that, on the ground, social actors themselves adhere to such stark distinctions in understanding themselves or their kin ties. One way to think about this is through the example of what anthropologists call 'fictive kin'.

What is the fictive in fictive kin?

Conventionally, 'fictive kin' are those kin with no 'biological' connection, that is, no connection through sexual procreation (conventionally, also, this connection through sexual procreation includes not only children conceived through heterosexual intercourse, but also heterosexual partners and their 'blood' relatives ('in-laws')). It is important to recognize that 'fictive' does not necessarily stand for 'false', but can simply mean 'made' (Carsten, 2004: 141). Fictive kin can be seen as kin who are 'adopted' – not simply adopted children, but others who are 'adopted' into a kin system. One relatively commonplace example is that of adults who are given the honorific 'auntie' and 'uncle' when addressed by children within a family. Another, perhaps more radical, example is that of gay kinship systems in the United States studied by Kath Weston (1991). Weston's work documents the significance of kin-type networks that are just as important and enduring as so-called 'real' (biological) kin. Her work shows how social actors in their own practices may challenge the distinction between 'nature' and culture', as cultural work transforms social categories (friendship) into (what is generally seen as) a 'natural' category (kin). Similarly,

Gerd Baumann's work in Southall, London, highlights the use of 'cousin' as an idiom among youth to denote a particular kind of relationship (Baumann, cited in Carsten, 2004). This is a relationship that – unlike friendship – does not cross religious divides. On the other hand, it is not necessarily based on 'blood ties'. Again, it is a category in which the natural and the cultural become fused. As Carsten notes in her commentary on this work,

> If . . . what anthropologists have been used to describing as 'fictive' kinship is asserted to be just as real as 'true' kinship, or if, in the Southall case, it is virtually impossible to establish the genealogical basis of cousin claims, then whose kinship is it? Schneider asserted that the primacy of biological ties in anthropological analyses of kinship arose from indigenous European and American folk assumptions [i.e. from the assumptions of anthropologists]. But it would appear that not all the natives adhere to these assumptions in the same way or to the same degree.
> (Carsten, 2004: 146)

Carsten is suggesting, in other words, that, while kin are always recognized according to some kinship logic, this logic may not in practice give primacy to 'blood', but may, as for the people in Weston's research, privilege endurance through time or, as in Baumann's ethnography, privilege shared 'community'. What is interesting about usage such as this is that it 'mixes up' nature and culture – what is given and what is made, as culture becomes made into 'nature' in the everyday kinship practices of (at least some) Westerners. In the next section I shall explore one final way in which kinship appears both to *rely on* ideas of nature and to confound those ideas. That section will explore the relationship between kinship and 'race'.

What does kinship do?

So far, I have discussed the significance of kinship in terms of claiming inherited or other 'blood' identities, and in the context of an arguably eroding or shifting nature/culture binarism. I want to broaden out the debate in this section to consider how kinship has been used both to justify and to legitimate inequalities based on identities – notably those of nation and 'race', and how it has been used to undermine those inequalities.

As I indicated in chapter 1, it is now generally agreed that 'race' has no basis in 'objective' natural 'facts', but is, rather, used to refer to identities forged within racist social relations. 'Race' is something made by racism, and it is racism which determines what gets to count as 'race'.

As such, race is another example (like kinship) of a cultural category produced *as if* founded in 'objective nature'. Nations, similarly, are cultural and social and political inventions, but they are often founded on an appeal to 'natural' categories – as, for example, in far-right appeals to 'authentic' Englishness (or Scottishness, or Frenchness, etc.; these terms can proliferate indefinitely).

Despite their 'invented' status, however, both 'race' and 'nation' are certainly real in their effects, and one way in which their 'reality' has been guaranteed is through references to kinship. Haraway (1997) shows that one significant way in which racism has worked is through appeal to kinship categories – through, for example, an appeal to the 'purity' of the bloodline, so that those characterized as 'polluting' the bloodline have been the source of suspicion and hatred. Hence prohibitions made by various states at various times on 'mixed' partnerships. It is worth noting, too, that the 'polluting' is always understood as coming from those who belong to dominated, 'othered' categories (white people have not generally been understood as polluting the bloodline of black people, for example). This is similar to the observation that while it is (believed to be) possible to be 'non-white', the category 'non-black' is not in general use (Fanon, 1967).

In this context, kinship stands as a system for organizing and legitimating specific forms of inequality, leading Haraway to write

> I am sick to death of bonding through kinship and 'the family', and I long for models of solidarity and human unity and difference rooted in friendship, work, partially shared purpose, intractable collective pain, inescapable mortality, and persistent hope. It is time to theorize an 'unfamiliar' unconscious, a different primal scene, where everything does not stem from the dramas of identity and reproduction. Ties through blood – including blood recast in the coin of genes and information – have been bloody enough already. I believe there will be no racial or sexual peace, no livable nature, until we learn to produce humanity through something more and less than kinship. (Haraway, 1997: 265)

There is plenty of evidence to support Haraway's point. Even a glance at (for example) twentieth-century European history confirms her comment that 'ties through blood have been bloody enough'. The dissolution of the former Yugoslavia was accompanied by warfare in which blood/kinship ties were used as a justification for mass murder. More broadly, notions of relatedness are common means of distinguishing 'us' from 'them' and forging boundaries that include and (of course) similarly exclude (Hackstaff, 2004).

And yet, in terms of how it is *done*, there is also evidence to indicate that kinship can be used to *undo* those boundaries, to mark out their contingent nature. Katherine Tyler's (2005) ethnographic study of interracial kin relationships in the United Kingdom gives a rather different perspective than that found by looking solely at the *rhetoric* of kinship. While discourses of racial 'purity' are often woven through notions of kinship – for example, in legal or social prohibitions on intermarriage, Tyler's research participants used the language of kinship to speak about and often to celebrate new kinds of identity that defy such racist notions of 'purity'. Far from using kinship to justify the status quo, these women – all of whom were part of interracial families – described using the 'raw materials' of kinship to forge *new* kinds of identity. While they frequently conceptualized kin ties in biological and essentialist terms, they did not suggest that such ties were fixed, and indeed they combined biological and cultural elements to embed themselves in kin systems. Further, these women's negotiation of kin ties and kin identities were bound up with anti-racist strategies, particularly in the context of bringing up their children to value their identities and to deal with racism.

For example, Tyler writes of one woman who had been adopted as a baby by a white family,

> As a child Sandra used to say that she was 'white' because she was not 'brought up' by a black family. While others identified her as 'black', an assumption that rests upon the folk belief that phenotype signals 'just' black or 'just' white biological parentage. It is only when Sandra's knowledge of her interracial family becomes melded with her inheritance of black cultural knowledge from her birth father, friends and neighbours . . . that she feels 'reborn' as an interracial woman. Thus her knowledge of her genetic 'origins' becomes a 'coding for ethnicity' when it is intersected with her inheritance of cultural knowledge and social relationships across the colour-lines, without which her interracial parentage and 'origins' do not make much sense. (Tyler, 2005: 486)

Again, we come back to the active 'working up' of identities based within kin systems. This working up defies any easy notions of 'natural' genetic identity. Not only are kin simply those we recognize as kin, but kinship *identity* is based on what we know and recognize. For the women in Tyler's study, racial identities are made on the basis of their knowledge and relationships which enable them to *interpret* their kin ties. They are not simply founded in 'blood'. As Marilyn Strathern (1988) notes, people acquire identities through knowing what to *make* of their identities. In many ways, this returns us to a contemporary concern with genealogical investigation. In such investigation, people recognize kin and recognize themselves in kin. As such, they are *producing* an identity at once unique and collective. Karla Hackstaff argues,

> Doing genealogy cannot be more faithfully characterized as connecting or disconnecting, including or excluding, elevating the social or the biological, promoting individualism or collective meaning. It is all of these. Boundaries are sustained and/or redrawn and inequalities are both challenged and reproduced by doing genealogy. (Hackstaff, 2004: 25)

Concluding remarks

I have argued in this chapter that kinship appears to tie us firmly in to the biological and the natural, but, at the same time, it defies those categories. For one thing, it always takes work, both the work of recognizing kin and the work of producing identities based on those kin. For another, nature itself is being reconfigured in understandings of kinship, so that what get to count as 'natural' ties are culturally imagined. The next chapter picks up some of the themes I have mentioned here: the ways in which 'expert' knowledges produce self-understandings, self-scrutiny and, ultimately, self-governance.

4 Becoming ourselves: governing and/through identities

Introduction

In the contemporary West, it is hard to avoid the idea that the self is a project to be worked on. Reality television shows routinely feature 'makeovers' of the body and the mind, or involve experts scrutinizing the lives of people in an effort to tell them how to deal with their children, partners or pets. Shows like *Oprah* draw on the old idea of the confessional to air the contemporary 'sins' of failure to commit, excessive drinking, drug-taking, violence, infidelity and so on. Their sins having been aired and subject to opprobrium by the studio audience, participants are urged to confront their shortcomings and to make the secular equivalent of an act of true repentance, helped along by those contemporary secular priests – therapists and counsellors. The self-help section of bookshops groans with books on how to change your self in pursuit of more success at work/in sexual relationships/with your children. All of this is, almost always, presented as freeing: there is a powerful subtext that changing ourselves involves throwing off the shackles of repression placed on us by various others or simply by 'society'. And above all, the goal held up by these various cultural forms is 'autonomy'. Free of ties to the past, and to others, we shall walk into a rosy future.

It might be asked, at least when everyone in the industrialized world lives a life of such phenomenal complexity that it is scarcely possible to live without dependence on networks of (known and unknown) others, what exactly 'autonomy' might look like. And it might further be asked why 'autonomy' has come to be understood as such a desirable state. Nevertheless, what Nikolas Rose calls 'the norm of autonomy' has become an orthodoxy in many discussions of identity. In this chapter I explore this issue of the self as a project and consider the argument that when we are most incited to be 'free', we are then *most* enmeshed in the workings of power. I shall discuss the relationship of the self to itself within a contemporary project of self-actualization, self-awareness and self-improvement. As several theorists have pointed out, autonomy has become a norm that ties us to a relentless self-scrutiny, in which we watch ourselves (and are watched by others) for signs, not of deviance and wrongdoing, but of unhealthy attitudes, desires and perceptions. That this is perceived as freedom rather than subjection to power is a result of a commonplace view of power as a repressive and denying force.

The alternative perspective – which envisages power as a force which works positively through our desires and our selves, which sees categories of subject as produced through forms of knowledge and which theorizes the relationship of the self to itself – owes a great deal to the work of the French philosopher Michel Foucault (1926–84). Numerous authors have taken up his insights, and although his work has not been universally well received, its impact is impossible to ignore. While it was only at the end of his life and work that Foucault *explicitly* concentrated on the self – and especially on what he calls 'the relationship of the self to itself' – he was, throughout his work, concerned to problematize conventional views of the self. So, in his work on prisons, on illness, on sexuality and so on, he systematically challenged a view of the self as endowed with intrinsic properties, whether forms of sexual preference, madness or illness. He said towards the end of his life that the question which had preoccupied him throughout his work was the question which has preoccupied Western philosophers since Kant – the question, 'what are we?' (Foucault, 1992).

His interventions in this area have numerous implications, but I want to highlight three major ways in which his work is both useful and influential: his view of the relationship between power and knowledge, his argument that particular kinds of identity are 'made up' within relations of power/knowledge, and his perspective on how the self works on itself, in what Foucault calls 'technologies of the self'. This last point has been particularly taken up by the British sociologist, Nikolas Rose, whose work I discuss later in the chapter.

Power/knowledge

As I noted earlier, power has conventionally been theorized as a prohibitive, denying force, working from the 'top down'. A powerful strand in Western Enlightenment philosophy has posited complex relationships between power, knowledge and identity, which have, in turn, proposed that the attainment of knowledge will free us from the workings of power. Such a view is summed up in the expression 'knowledge is power', in the suggestion that we can achieve power (and thus free ourselves from external powers) through achieving knowledge. This conceptualization assumes a true self which lies outside or beyond power (and, indeed, outside the social world). This self is knowable through reason and through self-reflection, and its actualization through self-knowledge will release us from the workings of power. Autonomy, in this formulation, is at the opposite pole to regulation and government, and, indeed, to the workings of power.

Foucault's work also links the three concepts of power, knowledge and selfhood, but in a wholly different way. He opposes the view that knowledge is power, arguing instead that one of the ways in which power works is through producing 'truths' about the world. These truths come to seem obvious, necessary and self-evident; they form part of the coherence of the social world and the place of the person within it.

Foucault argues that the West over the last 150 years or so has seen a gradual shift in the uses and forms of power. He argues that we have seen a move from *juridical or law-like power*, which uses the language of rights and obligations, to forms of *normalizing or regulatory power*, which uses the language of health, self-fulfilment and normality. If juridical power 'says' 'obey me or you will be punished', regulatory power 'says' 'obey so that you can be happy, healthy and fulfilled'. Juridical power uses the language of rights and obligations; it is an externally imposed form of power. Regulatory, disciplinary power uses the language of health, normality. It invokes forms of pleasure. It works, not through the imposition of taboos but through categorization, normalization and administration. It is a form of power which does not rely on external coercion, but in which we scrutinize, regulate and discipline our selves – the self comes to act *on* itself.

Regulatory power is dispersed throughout the social network rather than being concentrated in the hands of the state. Power is thus *exercised*; it is not owned. However, and as I discuss later in the chapter, it is not exercised equally by everybody, and while the state may not 'own' power, it does exercise it – often in ways that mask its power-like character.

It is not, Foucault argues, that the law has somehow 'disappeared': rather it is no longer the most significant modality of power. Regulatory power has come to saturate the social world: it is present in all appeals to self-fulfilment and self-improvement, whether of the mind or the body. In such appeals we are enjoined to be a particular type of person – happy, healthy, fulfilled and, above all, autonomous. We are enjoined to work on ourselves to make sure that we are this kind of person.

If such forms of address do not strike us as the workings of power, this is precisely because the conventional model of power as only a prohibitive and denying force makes it difficult to see other ways in which power works. But, for Foucault, power is at its most powerful when it is least repressive. Power works not just through denying, but through offering ways of being, forms of pleasure and so on. As he observes,

> If power were never anything but repressive, if it never did anything but say no, do you really think one would be brought to obey it? What makes power hold good, what makes it accepted, is simply the fact that it doesn't only weigh on us as a force that says no, but that it traverses and produces things, it induces pleasure, forms knowledge, produces discourses. It needs to be considered as a productive network which runs through the whole social body, much more than as a negative instance whose function is repression. (Foucault, 1980: 119)

If power is not only a forbidding and denying force, neither is it a force that conceals or distorts a 'truth', the revelation of which will free us from the workings of power. Rather, power and knowledge are bound together: the extension of power involves the production of knowledges by which people can be known and understood:

> We should abandon a whole tradition that allows us to imagine that knowledge can exist only where the power relations are suspended and that knowledge can develop only outside its injunctions, its demands and its interests . . . We should admit rather that power produces knowledge . . . that power and knowledge directly imply one another . . . there is no power relationship without the correlative constitution of a field of knowledge, nor any knowledge that does not presuppose and constitute at the same time power relations. (Foucault, 1979: 27)

As Tom Inglis neatly puts it, 'Power announces truth' (Inglis, 2003: 16). Its truths are forged on the basis of knowledge (*savoir*), but this refers not to knowledge about a set of facts, but rather to what might be termed *ways of knowing*, or, in Foucauldian terms, discourses. Discourses define what can be said and thought, and how these things can be said and thought. But this is about more than ideas, or words. Discourses are not simply representations, or ways of speaking; they are what Edward Said (1991: 10) calls 'epistemological enforcers', creating the rules of *what* can be said and thought about, and of *how* those things can be said and thought about. They can be seen as verbal and non-verbal ways of organizing the world, creating some ways of conceptualizing that are seen as axiomatically obvious and 'true', while others are outside sense.

The argument being made here is that certain things become 'true', not because of any intrinsic property of the statements themselves, but because they are produced from within authoritative, powerful positions, and they accord with *other* 'truth statements'. They are part of a system of knowledges. As a result they seem to be 'inevitable, unquestionable, necessary', as Ian Hacking puts it (1995: 4). Some knowledges are understood in this way, while others are outside 'sense'. To explain unhappiness, say, through claiming to have been cursed would be to put oneself outside the intelligibility norms of this time and place. To explain one's unhappiness with reference to a difficult childhood seems coherent and perhaps even obvious. This is because a view of childhood as the source of the self is an important way through which people in Europe and North America organize and make sense of the world. To reiterate: discourses are about *ways of knowing*.

Discourses form the intelligibility rules of a given culture and historical era. Hacking, in his commentary on Foucault's notion of power/ knowledge, refers to them in terms of 'depth knowledge' and argues,

> This 'depth' knowledge is more like a postulated set of rules that determine what kinds of sentences are going to count as true or false in some domain. The kinds of things to be said about the brain in 1780 are not the kinds of things to be said a quarter-century later. That is not because we have different beliefs about brains, but because 'brain' denotes a new kind of object in the later discourse, and occurs in different sorts of sentences. (Hacking, 1986: 30–1)

'The brain' becomes produced as an object of knowledge in different ways, depending on the historical, social and political context. So too with other categories – including, as we shall see, categories of human subject. From this perspective, what gets to count as 'true' is an effect, not of intrinsic properties of the knowledge itself; it is, rather, an effect of the social relations that produce them as true. In this sense, discourse is entirely different from ideology. While discourses are productive of social phenomena – of what counts as 'real' – the concept of ideology almost always presupposes a 'real' which is both beyond ideology and obscured by it (Barrett, 1991). To speak of ideology is to speak of the lies that *obscure* the truth, but to speak of discourses (in the Foucauldian sense) is to speak of the knowledges that *produce* the truth. Foucault saw his work as concerned with 'the politics of truth' and contrasted it with 'the economics of untruth'. That is, he replaces a concern with how we come to be governed by lies and untruth (as with ideology) with a concern with how we come to be governed by truths which are *made* true.

This is not to claim that discourse is fixed; there are always struggles for meaning and the fact that discourses change across time and place indicates that change is possible. But neither are they easily ignored or opted out of. It is simply not possible, in many cases, to speak or even to think 'outside the true'. But more fundamentally, perhaps, the kinds of knowledge produced within discourse do not simply concern sets of 'facts' about the external world, but are about what kinds of persons we are. Thus they are bound up with our sense of self. Hacking asks rhetorically,

> Does one feel different, has one a different experience of oneself, if one is led to see oneself as a certain type of person? Does the availability of a classification, a label, a word or phrase, open certain possibilities, or perhaps close off others? (Hacking, 2004: 285)

What this line of questioning opens up is the possibility that *who we (and others) are* is an effect of what we *know ourselves (and others) to be*, that knowledges have produced categories of person and that this is how we understand ourselves. I noted in the last chapter Strathern's argument that identity is produced through knowledge: what we are is what we know ourselves to be. This is similar to the Foucauldian precept that we are addressed, and address ourselves as, certain kinds of person, and through this process, we *become* that person. To explain this further, the next section considers Foucault's analysis of the creation of sexual subjects.

Making people up

A good example of categories of person being *produced* lies in Foucault's discussion of the figure of 'the homosexual' (Foucault, 1990).[1] Contemporary Westerners are accustomed to think of what is now called 'sexual preference' as being a deep-seated part of our

---

[1] Foucault's discussion concentrates on male homosexuals, but similar moves created the category 'lesbian'.

identity as persons. Sex is not understood simply as something we do; it is taken to indicate something we *are*. Foucault, however, argues that this way of bringing together sexual desire and identity is relatively recent. It is clear that people have always engaged in same-sex genital activity, and in some places and times this has been institutionalized (at least between men). But it is only in the late nineteenth century that we see 'the homosexual' appear as a *category of subject*. In this sense 'homosexuals' (and of course their counterparts, 'heterosexuals') did not exist before the nineteenth century.[2] Before that, same-sex sexual activity was simply something anyone might do – an act, like fornication or adultery, generally punishable either by church or state, but not indicating a category of subject:

> As defined by the ancient civil or canonical codes, sodomy was a category of forbidden acts; their perpetrator was nothing more than the judicial subject of them. The nineteenth-century homosexual became a personage, a past, a case history, and a childhood, in addition to being a type of life, a life form, and a morphology, with an indiscreet anatomy and possibly a mysterious physiology. (Foucault, 1990: 43)

So what occurred at this time was the amalgamation of a series of acts into an identity, a person. In this way we might say that the homosexual person was 'made up'. Along with this, of course, the heterosexual person had, similarly, to be 'made up', since homosexuality would have no meaning without an 'opposing' category. In large part, this production of sexual subjects came about through the intervention of a new pseudo-science of sexology, whose practitioners engaged in a minute categorization of sexual practices, themselves based on the confessions of people who had newly become sexual subjects. These new categories of knowledge *produced* what they claimed to be *describing*: new categories of person.

It is important to emphasize, also, that with these new forms of knowledge came new forms of power. Foucault frames his argument in the context of his refutation of what he calls the 'repressive hypothesis'. This hypothesis is a familiar one; it is frequently rehearsed and tends to be taken for granted as obvious. Its basic premises are as follows: the Victorian era was one in which sex was repressed and unspoken; we are now – and happily – more emancipated than our Victorian forebears and have effectively thrown off the shackles of

---

[2] There is some dispute over whether Foucault's dating of this move is correct (see, e.g., Weeks, 1987). But the point I want to make here is that at some point there was no distinctive category 'homosexual'; and now, of course, there is.

power that go with sexual repression. We can, for example, more easily talk about sex and this is a good thing, since such ability to speak indicates a freedom from the shackles of repression.

While Foucault states that he is not interested in proving this repressive hypothesis wrong, he is certainly concerned to show its inadequacies. For example, the nineteenth century, far from being a period of silence around sex, witnessed a 'discursive explosion' in which sex began to be spoken of in new ways. With the rise of 'reason' and rationality, sex was increasingly to be spoken of in rationalist, 'scientific' terms, involving minute classifications:

> Rather than a massive censorship, beginning with the verbal proprieties imposed by the Age of Reason, what was involved was a regulated and polymorphous incitement to discourse. (Foucault, 1990: 34)

If Foucault wants to challenge the idea that sex was silenced in the nineteenth century then, equally, he wants to challenge the idea that we now enjoy unparalleled sexual freedom. Or, more fundamentally, he wants to challenge the belief that an apparent freedom indicates an absence of power and control. The newly invented category 'homosexual' arose out of a broader interest in, and concern with, 'sexuality', which began to be a thing in itself, rather than simply a set of acts or bodily sensations. And with this came new forms of scrutiny as new forms of expertise were produced. With new forms of expertise come new 'experts', whose authority derives not from the church or the crown, but from the precepts of rational science (Rose, 1991). Such experts watched for signs of sexual health and sexual deviance. While the creation of a distinct sexual 'subject' has clearly been a source of affirmation and empowerment for some, it is, equally, a way in which we are scrutinized (and, increasingly, scrutinize ourselves) for signs of abnormality or unhealthiness. Despite important changes, we live with this legacy, although, as I discuss below, the legacy goes much further than sexual identity to extend into every area of our lives and identities.

Technologies of the self

One way in which power works, according to this perspective, is through categorizing people in terms through which they come to understand themselves. In this sense, subjectivities and identities are created within regimes of power/knowledge. Certainly, we have bodily and emotional sensations, we live, we die, we get sick, we grieve, and so on, but the ways in which we understand these things – and the ways in which we organize them to produce particular kinds of identity – is another matter.

In explaining the relationship of the self to itself, Foucault uses the concept of subjectivation (*assujetissement*):

> There are two meanings of the word subject: subject to someone else by control and dependence, and tied to his own identity by a conscience or self-knowledge. Both meanings suggest a form of power which subjugates and makes subject to. (Foucault, 1982: 212)

Through subjectivation, people become tied to specific identities: they become *subjects*. But also they become *subject-ed* to the rules and norms engendered by a set of knowledges about these identities. They take up subject-positions – specific ways of being – available within discourse, understanding themselves according to a set of criteria provided by the experts whose authority derives from rationality and 'reason'. As Judith Butler comments,

> As a form of power, subjection is paradoxical. To be dominated by a power external to oneself is a familiar and agonizing form that power takes. To find, however, that what 'one' is, one's very formation as a subject, is in some sense dependent on that power is quite another. (Butler, 1997: 1–2)

For Foucault, the relationship of the self *to* itself – how individuals act on themselves – what he was to call technologies of the self – is an increasingly important form that power takes in the contemporary world. We constantly act upon ourselves to be a certain type of subject; we have little choice but to be tied in to a kind of project of the self, in which the self becomes something to be worked on – not just the sexual subjects I discussed earlier, though we can hardly now think of ourselves as anything other than 'having' a certain form, or certain forms, of 'sexuality'. We are subjected subjects across as many forms of identity as we have: as 'parents', 'children', 'workers', 'students', 'citizens' and so on. In earlier work on mothering (Lawler, 2000) I argued that, while women have obviously always had children, the category 'mother' takes on particular meanings depending on the meanings and definitions given to the category 'child'. This latter category, in turn, is defined and given meaning according to the specific political and social preoccupations of its context. I noted there that women as mothers are subject to the gaze of those professionals – health visitors, doctors, social workers and so on – whose job it is to ensure that they are getting it right. But more than this, they increasingly scrutinize *themselves* for signs of pathology. They act – indeed must act – on themselves. In taking up the subject-position 'good mother' (and who would want to be a bad mother?) they are *subjected* to a range of discourses which specify what the good mother is. They must, then, try to approximate that discursive figure (knowing that if anything goes wrong in their children's lives, they will be blamed). They are brought into being as maternal subjects, only to be subjected to sets of authoritative knowledges. The power at work here is at work through their desires, not in spite of them.

All of this has a wider application; not only in cultural products such as the self-help books mentioned earlier, but also in counselling, radio phone-ins and advice columns in newspapers and magazines, we are enjoined to be a certain type of person in order to be normal, healthy, self-fulfilled. We may go through pain to achieve this, but the assumption is that the pain will have been worth it. So, in not (apparently) being regulated, contemporary Westerners are increasingly regulating themselves. According to Foucault, modern Western forms of government increasingly operate on the basis of managing populations, rather than punishing them; the demand is for 'normality' rather than obedience to a sovereign power. Hence 'techniques of normalization' have become the preferred means of government. This is what Foucault terms 'governmentality', a specific usage and form of power in which populations are managed through classification and categorization. In which, in Butler's gloss,

> [T]he tactics characteristic of governmentality operate diffusely, to dispose and order populations, and to produce and reproduce subjects, their practices and beliefs, in relation to specific policy aims. (Butler, 2004b: 52)

I return to this issue later, when I discuss the role of the state in governmentality. I turn next to a discussion of the specific kinds of knowledge at work in contemporary Western conceptualizations of the self – and hence to a discussion of the knowledges at work in power/ knowledge.

Psy knowledge, expertise and authority

If, as Foucault argues, selves are produced in relations of power/ knowledge, what kinds of knowledge are at work? Increasingly significant in this context is the matrix of knowledges which produces truths about the self and its relations with others and which has been termed the 'psy complex' (Ingleby, 1985; see also Rose, 1991). The reference here is to knowledges generated through medicine, psychology, psychiatry, pedagogy and so on, which several commentators have seen as gaining ascendance in the contemporary world, to such a degree that they inevitably inform the self-perceptions and self-consciousness of people living in the contemporary West.

Psy knowledges are not confined to professional practice or statements within their own fields, but 'escape' from their specialist enclaves (Fraser, 1989) to inform the workings of other types of professionals (social workers, teachers, health visitors, counsellors and so on), and to inform, too, a host of fields which are currently 'growth markets' in Western cultures – self-help literature, 'personal growth', childcare advice. And, significantly, these knowledges are reiterated in the minutiae of daily life – in doctors' surgeries, on chat shows, on 'the radio call-in, the weekly magazine column' – and inform the relationship of the self to itself, through 'the unceasing reflexive gaze of our own psychologically educated self-scrutiny' (Rose, 1991: 208). The self is increasingly becoming a project to be worked on, in pursuit of the 'real self'.

Psy's knowledges are endlessly repeated across a range of sites, and, as we shall see, they are embedded in law and other state processes. This makes them particularly intractable. The knowledges generated by psy are not normally represented as *theories*, open to contestation, but as truths about 'human nature', to such a degree, Nikolas Rose claims, that 'it has become impossible to conceive of personhood, to experience one's own or another's personhood, or to govern oneself or others without "psy" ' (Rose, 1996: 139).

Psy governs through using regulatory or normalizing power – not working in spite of our desires, but through them – and generating specific kinds of desires in the first place. The history of this move goes back at least 150 years. Rose traces the rise of what he calls 'technologies of responsibilization' in which the home on the one hand was celebrated as the counterweight to government, the place where individual passions were to be invested, and, on the other, was designated as a place for moral training – especially the moral training of children. The home came to be the place where an ethic of good health and morality was fostered – and this was articulated on to a so-called 'public' ethic of social order and public hygiene.

Rose argues that the 'liberal' type of government emerging at this time ascribes a key role to experts – first doctors but then a host of others – who can specify ways of conducting private affairs. Their authority comes not from God or the crown, but because the pronouncements they make – and the behaviour they set down – is understood as rational and true.

For Rose, a whole set of ways of governing at this time – not just the role assigned to the home, but the educational curriculum, public welfare, designs of work spaces – brought about a new kind of subject. I noted in chapter 2 Rose's argument that the teaching of English literature in schools was introduced, in part, to enable the child to become aware of internal states, and to provide a language for speaking about them. In short, he says, 'they would actually create new civilized sensibilities' (Rose, 1999: 78). More recently, the introduction of 'circle time' into British primary schools can be seen as a means of encouraging particular sensibilities in young children: encouraging them to reflect on 'interior' states and to express those states and feelings in the company of others. 'Circle time' typically involves children sitting in a circle and throwing a small object such as bean bag. Whoever catches the bean bag must begin a sentence beginning 'I feel . . .'. According to at least one commentator (Clark, 1998), circle time is an important (and child-centred) procedure in training children to develop as moral beings.

'Circle time' is one example of 'child-centred' pedagogy and, as such, is usually seen as (and is represented as) a manifestation of freedom, rather than power. However, it can equally be seen as a means of regulating and governing children precisely through engendering certain forms of desire and ways of being. Through such interventions children can be seen as learning to be inner-focused persons: discipline then (ideally) becomes a matter of encouraging such inner-directedness as a means of conformity to social norms. It is worth noting, however, that children themselves may subvert such procedures in interesting ways. My daughter, when at primary school, reported a child in 'circle time' finishing the 'I feel . . .' sentence with '. . . like chicken tonight' (echoing an advertising jingle popular at the time). I've often wondered what the teacher made of this small act of subversion. But the story serves as a reminder that people subjected to psy knowledges do not necessarily wholeheartedly embrace them. Indeed, as Foucault argues, power is always accompanied by resistance.

The norm of autonomy and the scrutiny of the soul

As I noted earlier, Rose argues that we now live in a psychotherapeutic society, in which the self is understood as an inner state, to be sought out, understood and actualized. Rose's concern is not to show that this is the latest manifestation of a narcissistic, self-regarding and introspective culture (contrast Lasch, 1991). Indeed, he suggests that we are rather stuck with this, such that it is impossible to understand and know ourselves *without* the discourses of 'psy'. It is not a case of conforming to one particular, dominant or authoritative version of psy; as Elliott and Lemert (2006) rightly state, there are competing approaches in therapy, and people entering therapy are generally aware that they are, in some sense, 'choosing' one version. Rose's concern lies less with the consulting room and more with a wider culture in which, notwithstanding different therapeutic approaches, the concerns shared by various forms of therapy – notably a reflection on interior states as a cure for all kinds of ills – have entered numerous areas of the social world – and not as theories, but as 'truths' about 'human nature'. I return to this issue below.

Rose's main concern is to show how a psychotherapeutic culture, while stressing autonomy as a norm, actually ties us more closely to the workings of power. Foucault was concerned with the ways in which sex – in its so-called normal and abnormal manifestations – became an axis around which people's selves and behaviours could be judged; Rose suggests that this focus has broadened so that now it is autonomy, rather than sexual 'normality', that is the goal:

> [I]t is important to recognize what is at issue in these therapeutic technologies of knowledge and power – no longer sex, not even pathology, but our autonomous selves. (Rose, 1991: 245)

The norm of autonomy includes financial/economic autonomy, so that, as Fraser and Gordon note, 'there is no longer any self-evidently good adult dependency in post-industrial society' (Fraser and Gordon, 1994: 324). But it has also come to be seen as a property of the person, so that dependency or a lack of autonomy has come to indicate a faulty type of personality. 'Dependency' has shifted its meaning from its pre-industrial usage as a term that denoted structural relations of dependency to its contemporary usage as a term that suggests personal pathology. With the intensification of this shift in the mid-to-late twentieth century comes an intensification of an emphasis on 'autonomy' as a goal to be achieved through adhering to the strictures of psy expertise, and through watching and monitoring ourselves through the government of the soul:

> The government of the soul depends upon our recognition of ourselves as ideally and potentially certain sorts of person, the unease generated by a normative judgement of what we are and could become, and the incitement offered to overcome this discrepancy by following the advice of experts in the management of the self. (Rose, 1991: 11)

In support of his argument, Rose cites the growth in psychological and similar forms of expertise, not only in specialist enclaves such as hospitals and universities, but in self-help books, magazine columns, radio phone-ins, and so on. There seems little doubt that these ways of understanding the self have proliferated: even a cursory look at the 'self-help' section in a bookshop shows a remarkable array of texts, all of which have a surprisingly similar message: that we need to 'be ourselves' (who else could we be?) and, as part and parcel of this being or becoming ourselves, we need to be autonomous: free from the conscious or unconscious impositions of parents, lovers and (less frequently) children (Hazleden, 2003, 2004).

We might ask how autonomy came to be seen as a goal that is both *possible* and *desirable*. Nevertheless, the goal or ideal of a psychological autonomy is one that seems to have so successfully passed into the language that it is scarcely questioned. This, for Rose, is the primary way in which we have come to be governed. While the discourses of psy present themselves as offering freedom and liberation, they tie us ever more closely to a project of the self and, as such, they are an integral part of contemporary Western mechanisms of governance.

Foucault argues that, beginning in the eighteenth century and properly developing in the nineteenth, four major areas of sexual and social concern emerged in Europe (see figure 4.1). These were four 'specific mechanisms of knowledge and power centering on sex' (Foucault, 1990: 103), four processes through which sex began to be governed: a hystericization of women's bodies, a pedagogization of children's sex, a socialization of procreative behaviour, and a psychiatrization of perverse pleasure. Each of these axes of concern gave rise to a specific sexual subject: we might say that these subjects were *produced* within the specific relations of power/knowledge analysed by Foucault. Once again, relations of power/knowledge *create* what they claim to be (merely) *describing*.

In his play on Foucault's typology, Rose argues that, while these concerns have not disappeared, they have been displaced or augmented by wider concerns, which centre on the goal of autonomy and on four new principal sets of concerns:

a subjectification of work;
a psychologization of the mundane;
a therapeutics of finitude; and
a neuroticization of social intercourse.

Figure 4.1. Foucault's strategic unities and sexual subjects.

Strategic unity	Effects	Sexual subject
A hystericization of women's bodies	Female body as saturated with sexuality, as rightly under the control of medical science, and as responsible for regulating the social and familial realms.	The hysterical woman
A pedagogization of children's sex	Children as prone to indulge in sex, but this sex as dangerous.	The masturbating child
A socialization of procreative behaviour	Economic, political and medical regulation of the fertility of couples.	The Malthusian couple
A psychiatrization of perverse pleasure	Definition of sexual pleasure as a distinct biological and psychical instinct, subject to clinical analysis, defined as normal or abnormal, with corrective mechanisms to ensure its normality.	The perverse adult

Source: Foucault, 1990: 104–5; table adapted from Smart, 1985: 99.

A subjectification of work

In which work is understood as significant in terms of the identity it confers and the feelings experienced by the worker. Hence work is increasingly understood around notions of success and failure understood not primarily in economic terms but in terms of therapeutic values of fulfilment. These understandings are augmented by 'the correlative extension of the therapist into the organization of work, and of problems of work into the field and concern of all therapeutic activity' (Rose, 1991: 244).

A psychologization of the mundane

In which the normal, everyday occurrences – which might once have been seen as exigencies – come to be understood as 'life events'. In this way they are seen to have a potentially transformative role in a life and in the story of a life. Events such as marriage, childbirth, debt, house purchase and so on become moments that crystallize the extent to which we are properly 'coping' and 'adjusted'. To the extent that we are not, they are moments at which the underlying causes of such a lack ought to be sought out. Furthermore,

> Such events become the site of a practice that is normalizing, in that it establishes certain canons of living according to which failure may be evaluated. It is clinical in that it entails forensic work to identify signs and symptoms and interpretive work to link them to that hidden realm that generates them. It is pedagogic in that it seeks to educate the subject in the art of coping. It is subjectifying in that the quotidian affairs of life become the occasion for confession, for introspection, for the internal assumption of responsibility. (Rose, 1991: 244)

A therapeutics of finitude

In which grief, frustration and disappointment at the limits of life – from the ending of relationships to the ending of life itself – are reworked as issues of normality and pathology. These feelings are now understood as both dangerous and opportunities; they are dangerous because they may reveal (or form) problems, but they are also seen as opportunities because they are opportunities for personal growth, even in the face of pain. It is, of course, the latter that is assumed to be the desired goal in dealing with such situations, and indeed with the whole of life.

A neuroticization of social intercourse

In which relationships of various kinds have come to be understood as key elements in both personal well-being and social competence. Social ills become understood in terms of problems stemming from the ways in which we interact with others: the root of such ills and of various forms of 'failure' connected with them is, in turn, assumed to be rooted in problems in the early parent–child relationship:

> Therapists will take charge of this domain of the interpersonal, knowing its laws, diagnosing its ills, prescribing the ways to conduct ourselves with others that are virtuous because they are both fulfilling and healthy: in a reverse movement, the language of relationships will come to define our very conception of ourselves. (Rose, 1991: 245)

Across these four dimensions of the therapeutic, we see the production of a particular kind of self. Ideally, it is held, this self should be autonomous: self-actualizing, exercising choice (not to choose is to be less of a person), and a project to be worked on. The therapeutic, for Rose, operates on the basis of a logic of choice (we can choose, or not, to take up the chances available to us and become more 'autonomous' and more 'ourselves'; it is assumed, however, that we *ought* to so choose). It generates specific kinds of desire (particularly the desire for self-development, which is now marked as an unmediated Good Thing). It guides those desires, showing the best way to self-development. And finally, when it all goes wrong and the dream fails to materialize, it is the therapeutic itself – in the form of therapists and counsellors – which offers the remedy to the anxieties that emerge *because* it has all gone wrong.

So, for Rose, we are increasingly subject to a therapeuticized culture, in which social ills become personal problems to be resolved through therapy. It is not even necessary to receive therapy as such, because the culture is filled with this kind of understanding of the self and its relationships with others.

> In the new modes of regulating health, individuals are addressed on the assumption that they *want to be healthy*, and enjoined to freely seek out the ways of living most likely to promote their own health . . . Individuals are now offered an identity as consumers – offered an image and a set of practical relations to the self and others. (Rose, 1999: 86–7, emphasis in original)

All of this relies on and rests on the premise that we are certain kinds of self – deep selves for whom events are both problem and opportunity, for whom working on the self will bring reward and fulfilment. For Rose, the effect is actually to *produce* us as this kind of self. Indeed, this kind of understanding of the self, although not total, is so normalized that to question it can be very counter-intuitive. It also looks like a liberal and empowering model. But, for Rose, this is because it works through the rhetoric of freedom, not because it really is freeing. He argues that we are now obliged to live in a project of our own identity, and

> The irony is that we believe, in making our subjectivity the principle of our personal lives, our ethical systems, and our political evaluations, that we are, freely, choosing our freedom. (Rose, 1991: 11)

The state of the therapeutic

I noted above that, within a Foucauldian schema, power is dispersed throughout the social network rather than concentrated in the hands of the state. This does not mean, however, that the state does not exercise power. Indeed, for Foucault, the state is 'vitalized' by governmentality. Yet, as Butler (2004b) notes, this does not mean that the 'old' order of sovereignty and juridical power is *devitalized* at the same time. One obvious way in which states continue to exercise power is through the workings of law – in judgments in the courts. But states can also be seen as exercising regulatory, normalizing power through their deployment of expertise, and this exercise of power is less obviously power-*like*, since, as I noted earlier, it works in and through our desires and not in spite of them: it does not simply say 'no', but enjoins us to be certain types of selves (see Smart, 1989).

There are various ways in which state institutions harness expertise in this way, but perhaps the clearest and most sustained use lies in the state's use of expert knowledges around the figure of 'the child'. As I noted above, we can be seen to be 'made up' as certain kinds and categories of person – the gay man, the straight woman, the mother, the grieving relative, etc. – and then *addressed* as that kind of person. From this perspective, 'child' is also a category produced within discourse. To say this is not to deny that children are born physically, emotionally and psychologically dependent. It is, rather, to point to the ways in which children are attributed specific characteristics and (especially) needs and to point out that contemporary Western conceptualizations of the child are neither inevitable nor universal.

There is a growing body of work on the sociology of childhood that addresses these matters and that highlights the ways in which the figure of the child is a focus for various social anxieties and panics (see, for example, Steedman, 1995; Jenks, 1996; James et al., 1998; Meyer, 2007). It is not my intention here, however, to go into this set of debates – important though it is. Rather, I am concerned to highlight the ways in which one aspect of childhood – a particular set of 'needs' attributed to the child – is used as a means of regulating parents (especially mothers) and their children through the imposition of norms.

Valerie Walkerdine and Helen Lucey (1989) provide an analysis of the relations between expert knowledges around child-rearing, the state regulation of families (especially mothers and children) and the production of the good, ordered society. A major part of their project lies in the analysis of the links between the political projects of modern liberal democracies and the types of knowledge engendered by contemporary and recent psychological research. They argue that, for modern liberal democracies to function effectively, they require citizens who believe themselves to be 'free', who believe that equal opportunities are open to all, and whose demands on society are 'reasonable' – that is, they can be met without any significant demands being made on the status quo. How are such subjects to be produced?

Walkerdine and Lucey argue that responsibility for the production of such 'reasonable' citizens has come to rest with parents, and especially with mothers. While of course fathers also do childcare, the bulk of childcare continues to be carried out by mothers. Further, 'mother' and 'father' are not considered to be the same kind of parent within the expert developmental literature. Sensitivity is particularly required of mothers rather than fathers. Often it seems that it is enough for fathers simply to be *there*.

Hence mothers (in particular) ultimately become the guarantors of democracy, and democracy is held to be produced 'in the kitchen'. The state takes an explicit interest in ensuring that children become the 'right' kind of citizens, and it does this primarily through regulating parents. This is not achieved primarily through coercive measures but through the harnessing of parents' own desires. To be a 'good parent' is to follow the expertise of childcare advice. If things go wrong, this is not assumed to be a problem in the advice itself, but in the way the mother or father carried it out – generally, problems in the mother's or father's own self.

To the end of ensuring that children develop the 'right' kinds of selves, parents are enjoined to make learning into 'play', and not to make their own authority visible, but rather to appeal to 'reason'. Yet no one proposes that children should simply be left to do what they want: rather, mothers and fathers should regulate them, but this regulation should be invisible. So, instead of 'because I say so', parents should instead invoke reason and 'rightness'. In this way the child is supposed to grow up rational and reasonable. States employ numerous professionals, from health visitors and teachers to social workers, to monitor and regulate children and their parents in accordance with these forms of expertise. Certainly, it might be objected that social workers, for example, only intervene when children are seen to be at risk: but once children have come to the attention of social services, every aspect of their parents' parenting is under scrutiny. But more to the point, perhaps, the 'ideal', the norm, is that mothers and fathers should regulate themselves, scrutinizing their own behaviour through the lens of psy knowledges.

In this and a variety of other ways, parents, especially mothers, are regulated and monitored – albeit in ways that suggest themselves as liberating – the better to engender 'autonomy' in their children. Social problems, from educational failure to crime and delinquency, are pre-sented as the outcome of poor parenting (cf. Furedi, 2004). Parents become the guarantors, not only of the 'good child', but also of the 'good society'. In this way, *structural* inequalities become reduced to *feel-ings*, and oppression and exploitation are hidden. Contrary to 'equal opportunities' rhetoric, the *belief* that you can succeed will not over-turn a social system in which only a minority *can* 'succeed'. Hence engendering a sense of autonomy in children – the belief that they can do anything – will not make the structural barriers to some children's achievement go away. No amount of sensitive parenting will change structural inequalities, and, for Walkerdine and Lucey, this autonomy is illusory:

> [S]uccessful parenting rests on creating an illusion of autonomy so con-vincing that the child actually believes herself to be free. We believe that this fiction, this illusion of autonomy, is central to the travesty of the word 'freedom' embodied in a political system that has to have everyone ima-gining themselves to be free the better to regulate them. (Walkerdine and Lucey, 1989: 29)[3]

Certainly the state retains its ability to use coercive measures such as the removal of children or to direct legal sanctions against parents. But for the most part it operates through the 'friendly advice' of health visitors and similar professionals. And, increasingly, in the United Kingdom at least, even draconian sanctions are used alongside regu-latory elements such as 'parenting classes' for parents of children seen as deviant, in what Carol Smart (in a different context) has character-ized as a 'merger' between law and psy knowledges (Smart, 1989). The introduction into English and Welsh law of parenting contracts and parenting orders is one interesting example of such a merger.

Parenting orders were introduced in England and Wales under the Crime and Disorder Act 1998 and extended under the Anti-Social Behaviour Act 2003 and the Criminal Justice Act 2003 (there are similar arrangements in Scotland), and seem to represent a peculiarly British solution to the 'problem' of young people, particularly young people

---

[3] There is not space here to discuss it in detail, but Walkerdine and Lucey's analysis incorporates an important class analysis. They question the assumption that the kind of mothering carried out by white, middle-class mothers is by definition the 'right' kind, suggesting instead that all mothers will teach their children what they know of the world. The problem is not that working-class mothers are getting it wrong (as is so often suggested) but that their worlds are pathologized. For example, mothers are not supposed to teach their children that the world is hard, but for many working-class parents the world *is* hard.

who are seen to represent a threat (I am not aware of any direct equivalent elsewhere). Parenting orders can be given to parents whose children have committed a criminal offence, or have received an anti-social behaviour order (ASBO), a child safety order or a sex offender order. They are overseen by a youth offending team – a team which is made up of representatives from the police, the probation service, social services, health, education, drugs and alcohol workers, and housing officers.

Parenting contracts are voluntary, and there is no penalty for their breach, but if parents of children who are seen to be deviant do not co-operate with a youth offending team – if they do not agree to a parenting contract, in other words – they are likely to be subject to a parenting order. Parenting orders involve counselling and guidance, as well as the requirement to supervise and monitor their children to the satisfaction of the youth offending team. The parenting contract turns out not to be voluntary after all. The language of the circular outlining these changes (Home Office, 2004) is couched in terms of 'opportunities', 'parental skills' and so on – in the language of choice and opportunity, rather than the language of punishment. But if parents don't go along with these 'opportunities', it seems that punishment swiftly ensues. There is no room to refuse the terms in which the discourse is framed.

Identities then – the right and wrong ones, the ruly and the unruly, the reasonable and the unreasonable – have become a central concern of states. While, as I have indicated, the state continues to rely on juridical power and even on draconian methods of enforcing order, such methods tend to be used on those for whom the techniques of liberal, normalizing power are seen to have 'failed'. These are people who have the wrong kind of self. So 'terrorists', for example, are constituted as wholly different kinds of *person* to 'us' (where 'us' stands for the normal, responsible, autonomous citizen). Indeed the very naming *as* terrorists constitutes them as outside the norm. What becomes the object of scrutiny is not only what they *do*, but what they are (understood to be). In more mundane arenas of life, anti-social behaviour orders (ASBOs), parenting orders and so on can be seen in terms of a 'last resort' when appeals to autonomous, responsible personhood are seen to have failed. Again, the focus is on what people *are*:

> [S]trategies for the conduct of conduct increasingly operate in two distinct sectors. For the majority, expertise operated not through social planning, paternalism and bureaucracy, but in terms of a logic of choice, through transforming the ways in which individuals come to think of themselves,

through inculcating desires for self-development that expertise can guide and through claiming to be able to allay the anxieties generated when the actuality of life fails to live up to its image. Yet a minority remain outside this regime of civility. They are, no doubt, the 'usual suspects' – the lone parent, the juvenile delinquent, the school truant, the drug user, the homeless person, the alcoholic – but their problems are represented in a new way, and are hence amenable to new modes of intervention. The 'urban underclass' becomes a new way of codifying this socially problematic and heterogeneous population of anti-citizens – an amalgam of cultural pathology and personal weakness which is racialized in particular ways, spatialized within the topography of the city, moralized through a link with sexual promiscuity and the 'unmarried mother', criminalized through a propensity to drugs and lawlessness. (Rose, 1999: 88)

'The usual subjects' are doubly pathologized in that not only are they seen as failing to conform to the ideal of social order and contemporary social citizenship, but this failure is understood in terms of their own, personal, psychological failure. As Valerie Walkerdine (2003) has commented, recent political moves have replaced a grammar of exploitation with a language of individual psychology. As a result, social inequalities are now increasingly seen as inhering within the subjectivities of social actors; it is their very selves which are seen as 'wrong' or 'right', healthy or pathological. This is an odd form of identity politics, in which civil society is premised on the selves of citizens. The discourses of psy – apparently so inclusive and liberating – rest on the exclusion of outsiders who do not conform to psy's precepts and who can be blamed for states of affairs seen as undesirable.

While it is no doubt a mistake to try to read off political activism from theory, it is worth asking how, within this theoretical schema, change could be made to occur. As I noted above, Foucault makes it clear that resistance always accompanies power, but this is not a 'theory of resistance' on a grand scale as, for example, are Marxist theories of revolution. Nikolas Rose argues for an acknowledgement of acts of resistance in the 'little territories of the everyday' (Rose, 1999: 280), citing the feminist slogan, 'the personal is political', as an example of a mobilization of forms of resistance that occurs not only on the 'grand stage' of the political arena, but also in the quotidian detail of life.

It is clear that Foucault himself does not offer a straightforward theory of resistance as a way through this morass of being governed 'through the soul'. There is no straightforward path to take which would translate into the happy road to freedom. Having examined the 'truths' by which we are governed, the task is not then to search for other, truer, truths. For Foucault, the task is perhaps more difficult:

> My point is not that everything is bad, but that everything is dangerous, which is not exactly the same as bad. If everything is dangerous, then we always have something to do. So my position leads not to apathy but to a hyper- and pessimistic activism. I think that the ethico-political choice we have to make every day is to determine the main danger. (Foucault, 1983: 343)

In other words, the task is not to attempt to step *outside* the discourses that define the world and our places and identities within it; the political task, rather, is strategically and repeatedly to oppose the terms of certain discourses. Furthermore, we can never assume that an issue of power is 'dealt with' once and for all. This is important because, as Rose (1999) notes, resistances can be recuperated within the mainstream and used for quite different purposes from those originally intended. Hence the Foucauldian injunction to exercise ethico-political vigilance, in which the task is to watch for the fluctuating, rather slippery, workings of power and subjection.

Concluding remarks

I have tried to point to various ways in which the varying regulatory regimes identified by Foucault and Foucauldians can be incorporated by social actors, so that their schema of understanding become means of self-understanding. From this perspective, social relations are 'folded into' the self, so that, rather like a Moebius strip, the self is folded over on itself. What seem to be inner, interior states are simply aspects of subjectivity produced as such through relations of power/ knowledge. They do not 'belong' to the individual: rather the individual is produced as such through these relations. 'Identity' is too solid a concept for the rather 'emptied out' character of personhood used by Foucault and Rose. We need, instead, to think of attachments to various subject-positions ('mother', 'teacher', 'concerned citizen' – or, equally, 'rebel', etc.) in which we make investments. One problem with this perspective is that it is not always clear *why* people make such intense investments in some forms of self-understanding, and not in others, or, indeed, exactly how such understandings come to constitute the self. Ian Hacking, for example, comments,

> Foucault gave us ways in which to understand what is said, can be said, what is possible, what is meaningful – as well as how it lies apart from the

unthinkable and indecipherable. He gave us no idea of how, in everyday life, one comes to incorporate those possibilities and impossibilities as part of oneself. (Hacking, 2004: 300)

Perhaps Hacking overstates his case, but I agree that any sense of the 'how' – or the 'why' – of this incorporation is thin in Foucault's work. And perhaps for this reason some have tried to supplement his perspectives with psychoanalysis – a move of which Foucault himself would certainly have disapproved, since he saw psychoanalysis as part of the complex of interventions and knowledges through which people are governed.[4] In chapter 6 I discuss the work of Judith Butler, who attempts to use both psychoanalytic and Foucauldian perspectives in her work. The next chapter turns to psychoanalysis itself.

---

[4] This may have been because psychoanalysis enjoys an institutional status in France that it does not in the anglophone world. See Barrett, 1991.

5 I desire therefore I am: unconscious selves

Introduction

Psychoanalysis occupies an uneasy place in anglophone culture. On the one hand it is a source of fascination – so many films, for example, take psychoanalysis as their theme (from Hitchcock's *Spellbound* to Ramis' *Analyze This*, not to mention almost all of the Woody Allen oeuvre, or, in a televisual representation, *The Sopranos*). Other cultural forms give more than a nod to psychoanalytic concepts, using notions of the unconscious, of repression, of splitting of the self and so on (*Being John Malkovich, Wolf, Identity*). All of this would suggest that psychoanalysis occupies a central place in the culture. However, and on the other hand, psychoanalytic principles are frequently treated with ridicule. The status of psychoanalysis as a 'failed science' no doubt contributes to this. Psychoanalytic procedures are a long way from the experimental method, and this is often taken as *in itself* some kind of proof that it must be wrong. Yet in this it is hardly alone. A great deal of knowledge, even in the natural sciences, is generated from theoretical precepts rather than experiment. Psychoanalysis operates within its own terms of reference and is not amenable to 'proof' or 'disproof' in the usual sense. However, to reject it on those grounds would, in my view, be fundamentally mistaken. There are many theoretical perspectives with which we work within sociology (and other disciplines) that are not testable using 'scientific' methods. What we tend to look for in such theories are ways of understanding, appraising and interpreting the world. The point is not can we prove them? but are they useful to think with?

This chapter will consider what psychoanalysis might have to offer sociological theories of identity. Unlike many of the other theories discussed in the book (and, more generally, used within sociological analysis) psychoanalysis relies on the presupposition that identity formation is far from being a conscious activity. Indeed, when it is treated as a role-learning theory, it does start to look absurd: but it is not and was never intended to be such a theory. Importantly, however, psychoanalysis explains things that in many other theories are left unexamined or taken for granted – how we become gendered, why we desire one thing (or one sex) rather than another, why we envy, why we hate – all these and other difficult questions. The next section will discuss some of the foundational principles of psychoanalysis.

The 'dynamic unconscious'

'Psychoanalysis', writes Adam Phillips, is about 'the most ordinary things in the world' (Phillips, 1993: xi). It takes the everyday, the quotidian – people's everyday loves, fears and fantasies – and considers what such things tell us about those people. But while it looks at the ordinary, it does so through an extra-ordinary lens, so that its precepts seem counter-intuitive. Stephen Frosh reminds us that

> [W]hen Freud introduced the notion of a dynamic unconscious, he brought a demon into the modern world which will not let anything alone, but which continually disrupts the things we take for granted and subverts the things we take to be true. (Frosh, 1997: 242)

The rest of this chapter is concerned with this 'dynamic unconscious', and with the ways in which part of what forms our identity is largely unknown to us. I cannot hope to do justice here to the totality of Freud's work, let alone to the whole psychoanalytic corpus, so my aim is rather to consider some of the main strands in psychoanalytic theory, especially as they relate to how people develop gendered and sexualized identities, as well as how those identities affect our relationships with ourselves and with others.

Psychoanalysis starts with Sigmund Freud (1856–1939), although of course it does not end with him. Freud started out as a neuroscientist, and only gradually developed what he saw (at least initially) as an entirely new kind of science – one which would provide both an analysis of the human subject, and a means of curing some of the mental ills which trouble human subjects.

In developing psychoanalysis, Freud developed a model of the personality fundamentally at odds with those conceptualized within other fields developing at the time. This was the time that saw the start of the scientific study of the brain and gave rise to such oddities as phrenology. So while these fields were trying to make the personality transparent (through mapping it out through the brain – a legacy still with us) Freud was rendering it opaque. Both fields were attempting to map the human person/self – and both have made entirely different kinds of map.[1]

In considering psychoanalytic perspectives on identity, two questions arise. First, how far are Western understandings of selfhood informed by psychoanalytic accounts? Second, how adequate, in terms of explanation and interpretation, are the *analyses* of self and identity provided by psychoanalysis? This chapter is more directly concerned with the second of these questions than the first, but both are important.

Psychoanalytic precepts have, within Western cultures since the twentieth century, 'passed into the language', generating schemata of understanding from which few of us are immune. As Michèle Barrett puts it,

> [T]he insights of psychoanalysis with regard to the unconscious, repression, fantasy, sexuality and so on are not merely 'within the true' of psychoanalytic discourse, but play an important part in the way in which people in contemporary western societies now understand themselves . . . To say that we live in the west in a therapeutic culture, where people interpret, reflect upon and to some extent change their behaviour in the light of psychoanalytic ideas (and, for some, therapy) is not to say that these ideas are not 'true': it is to understand the contextuality of their truth. So it is not a case of being for or against psychoanalysis . . . but of recognising that in certain times and places – and I am now writing from one of them – psychoanalytic concepts are rooted in the culture. (Barrett, 1991: 115)

To an extent, then, psychoanalysis provides us with a means of structuring our personal narratives, so that, for instance, unhappy relationships or failure to achieve a goal may be rooted in our childhood relationships with our parents. It is not necessary that everyone undergoes analysis or therapy in order for these understandings to take effect, since, as I have suggested, this view of the world is found throughout the culture, from fiction and visual representations to advice columns in newspapers and magazines. In many ways we are all Freudians, or, at least, post-Freudians. As Paul Ricoeur (1989) has observed, in *analysing* the world, Freud *changed* the world. In conceptualizing human beings as governed by desires and fears of which we are only dimly aware, Freud, in an important sense, *made* us into those people. As a result it is almost impossible for contemporary Westerners to think of themselves as anything other than containing

---

[1] My thanks to Mariam Fraser for this observation.

some 'depth' – some element of the self which is not immediately accessible. We give primacy to childhood in the shaping of the self, and certain Freudian terms have passed into the language. Although 'sub-conscious' is not a Freudian term (as we shall see, Freud used the word 'unconscious', not subconscious, to refer to those parts of the self that are inaccessible), it is relatively common to hear people refer to 'sub-conscious' motives. In this they are invoking a relatively inaccessible part of the self, one that nevertheless manifests itself in certain types of behaviour. The notion of the Oedipus complex is in wide cultural cir-culation, even if it is not applied with much precision. Probably most of us are aware of the concept of a 'Freudian slip', in which someone utters what is in some sense forbidden to be said, but nevertheless speaks their real feelings and desires. Most forms of counselling and psychotherapy rely on the notion that there exist 'inner' states in the person, and that these inner states must be brought into the light, examined and unravelled.

All of this suggests that Freudian ideas have successfully colonized our notion of the person. But such ideas coexist with quite different, even antagonistic, conceptualizations of selfhood, so that, as I have suggested, twenty-first-century Westerners exist in a curious relation-ship with Freud and psychoanalysis in general. Freudian conceptual-izations of the self are fundamentally at odds with many of our most cherished beliefs – about autonomy, about agency, about rationality and so on. For example, in direct opposition to the notion that we are in control of the world, that it is persons who consciously shape events, psychoanalysis insists that we are not even in (conscious) control of our own lives. In contrast to the notion that the self has a privileged insight into itself, psychoanalysis proposes that we cannot really know ourselves. Against the belief that we act rationally, exer-cising 'choice' in the course of our lives, psychoanalysis proposes a dif-ferent kind of logic at work, one in which 'the ego is subject to the whims and fancies of desire' (Frosh, 1997: 71).

In short, psychoanalysis dethrones the subject. Freud himself pro-posed that psychoanalysis visited a 'narcissistic wound' upon human-ity (Freud, 1917a), that is, it forces humans to confront their lack of control, autonomy and sovereignty. This is a claim on a grand scale; Freud cites only two other 'narcissistic wounds': that which took place as a result of the Copernican revolution (when Copernicus showed that the earth rotates around the sun, and not vice versa) and the other the result of Darwinism (when Darwin removed humans' 'special' status among living things).

Freud, then, is proposing that psychoanalysis removes humans from their imagined place at the centre of the universe. Just as 'His Majesty the Baby' must suffer an individual wound when she or he realizes that she or he is not the only person in the mother's world, so a collective humanity ought to realize, Freud suggests, that we are not fully in control of our own lives, still less of the world around us. Freud writes,

> [T]hese two discoveries – that the life of our sexual instincts cannot be wholly tamed, and that mental processes are in themselves unconscious and only reach the ego and come under its control through incomplete and untrustworthy perceptions – these two discoveries amount to a statement that *the ego is not master in its own house* . . . No wonder, then, that the ego does not look favourably upon psychoanalysis and obstinately refuses to believe in it. (Freud, 1917a: 143, emphasis in original)

Perhaps because Freudian notions are threatening to many 'mainstream' conceptualizations of the self, Freud's work has been subject to massive revision – to such an extent, some would say, that what is really radical about his position has been lost. It is often claimed that what is most radical in Freud's work is lost along the way of its conversion to a normalizing discourse of psychotherapy – which tells us how we can be healthy and happy. In contrast, Freud's aim was not to make his patients happy, but to convert neurotic misery into ordinary unhappiness. Further, the Freudian paradigm is basically a fatalistic one: the traumas and crises of our life are inevitable, and probably the most psychoanalysis can offer is a level of self-understanding and an easing of psychic distress.

This position is fundamentally at odds with most contemporary forms of non-psychoanalytic therapy in which the goal is often to induce a greater adaptation to roles and norms. (This is especially the case with ego-psychology, an American version of psychoanalysis which is usually considered to have moved a long way from Freud's original insights.) In Freudian terms, adaptation to norms is usually the problem rather than the solution. Furthermore, for psychoanalysis, neurosis is normal (we are all 'neurotic') and symptoms such as anxiety, depression or extreme jealousy are, similarly, manifestations – albeit particularly vivid manifestations – of 'normal' psychic life.

If popular forms of the therapeutic modify and change Freudian insights, these insights are also subject to ridicule and dismissal. Psychoanalysis often provokes quite stark and extreme emotional reactions. Of course, psychoanalysis has its own explanations for this, since hostility to psychoanalysis can be seen within the psychoanalytic schema as *proof* of psychoanalytic premises. This is because such hostility can be seen as a defence mechanism against a *recognition* of the truth of psychoanalysis – the acknowledgement, for example, that perhaps we are not all we seem to be and that we are not in complete control of our lives. This is, of course, something of a circular argument and anyone unconvinced by psychoanalysis seems unlikely to be convinced by this particular argument. However, and as Frosh (1997) notes, while one might not want to adhere too strongly to a position which holds that resistance to a theory upholds its truth, 'one might nevertheless want to preserve the possibility that an unpopular theory might nevertheless be in some way "true" ' (Frosh, 1997: 63). It may indeed be unsettling to see the self as so contrary to the self of liberal humanism – as not the master of its own fate, not the author of its own actions.

Why psychoanalysis?

This brings me to the second question I posed earlier: that of how accurate or meaningful an analysis of identity is offered by psychoanalysis. What psychoanalysis offers sociologists (whether or not they choose to take it up) is an interpretive schema: it gives us a way to consider the place of fantasy, repression and desire in the formation of the self, and a way to understand the non-conscious, non-rational, emotional elements of identity. As Frosh notes, this kind of analysis is central to an understanding of the world, not outside of such an understanding. Further, 'rational understanding' *depends upon* the capacity to allow expression to unconscious and non-coherent aspects of identity (Frosh, 1997: 72). And Rosalind Minsky argues,

> If we can accept that there is evidence for a dimension of identity which is outside our conscious knowledge, we have to ask how it came into being. Psychoanalytic theory is the discourse which attempts to provide the answer to this question because, alone among discourses, it deals with the human subject's unconscious coming into being and the kind of events which constitute an individual's hidden, unrecorded history. It charts not what we normally call history – the history of consciousness, of social power and domination, the social construction of reality – but another kind of story. This is the important history of the individual's unconscious construction, which takes place inside the wider social or cultural context, but maps how an individual has reacted to the powerful currents of emotion in his or her own family and the presences and absences, both physical and emotional, within this family. (Minsky, 1996: 8)

This notion of personal history in a social context is absolutely key to an understanding of psychoanalysis. While it is often assumed to be 'all about sex', psychoanalysis is, rather, all about reconstructions of the past. As Adam Phillips notes,

> Sexuality matters because it is one's history at its most cryptically encoded. Family history shows up in one's most intimate exchanges with other people. The lost – the literal and more figurative losses from one's past – are never, in this view, quite as lost as one feared, or indeed hoped. (Phillips, 2007: 20)

In the rest of the chapter I shall discuss some key Freudian concepts and consider what they offer in terms of sociological understandings of identity, especially those of gender and sexuality. Clearly, there are other important perspectives than those of Freud, as well as other substantive areas on which psychoanalysis can and does throw light. However, for the sake of brevity and clarity, I will confine myself to this focus. The next section looks at what is probably *the* key psychoanalytic concept – that of repression.

The unconscious, repression and personality

What it is crucial to understand about psychoanalysis is that it operates with what Paul Ricoeur calls 'a hermeneutics of suspicion'. It looks beyond what is apparent, beyond the situation as it seems to be; it is suspicious of what is manifest. So, for example, an *apparently* stable and unitary identity 'masks' the division of the person into the ego – the partially conscious sense of 'I' – the superego – the social conscience – and the id – the wild, asocial part of the self, full of unrealized desires and interested only in the pleasure principle. This division is not a happy *ménage à trois*: rather, the ego must in some sense 'manage' the competing demands of id and superego. In this sense, the self is necessarily divided against itself, finding itself daily involved in unconscious struggles with competing desires and demands.

Persons are not, however, born with this tripartite personality structure. At birth, the neonate – 'a little animal' – is a bundle of bodily sensations and drives and is characterized by the impulses of the id. Its transformation into a more or less socialized being (and, as I shall argue later, we are only ever 'more or less' socialized) involves processes of repression which result in the development of the ego and the superego. At birth, the infant experiences merger: she or he cannot distinguish between 'me' and 'not me'. In short, she or he has no ego (nor indeed does she or he have a superego). How does this develop?

It is impossible properly to understand or to engage with Freud's work without an appreciation of the central place he gives to the unconscious and to processes of repression. The 'unconscious' is not so much a place as a concept. It is the term given by Freud to that part of the self which 'contains' repressed desires and fears. The unconscious is not directly knowable; however, it is manifest in obsessive–compulsive behaviour, in slips of the tongue ('Freudian slips'), in psychosomatic illnesses, in jokes and in dreams (the 'royal road' to the unconscious, according to Freud). The dreams, fantasies and desires that produce our characters and our identities are, from this perspective, not open to conscious reflection. For Freud, we *do* have a consciousness: that part of us that we can directly know, and on which we can reflect. We also have a pre-conscious: this is Freud's term for that aspect of the self which is not directly known and understood, but which can be brought to mind. Most of what makes up the self, however, is unconscious.

For Freud, 'the theory of repression is the cornerstone on which the whole structure of psycho-analysis rests' (1914: 16) and it is a concept that can *only* be thought through psychoanalysis (Freud, 1915: 146). It is through repression that we become properly human subjects, that we develop an ego and a superego, that we learn to identify with others at the same time as retaining a sense of who we are, that we develop a sense of justice (of which more later).

'The essence of repression lies simply in turning something away, and keeping it at a distance, from the conscious' (Freud, 1915: 147). Repression occurs when desires are 'forbidden'; for example, the child's desire to return to an infantile state, to a time before the child her- or himself realized that she or he had to share her or his mother with others, is a 'forbidden' desire, which the child unconsciously fears will bring punishment. It is therefore a desire that the child must repress from consciousness. Although the achievement of such desires would bring the child pleasure, they would also cause (even more) 'un-pleasure' – presumably because she or he would then risk parental disapproval and (in fantasy) even the loss of the parents altogether.

Repression is not equivalent to 'forgetting': it is an active, dynamic process. While it begins in early childhood, it is never achieved once and for all but must be repeatedly achieved. This is an *inevitable* process, not dependent on what the parents teach the child, but something that will and must happen. Although there have been various attempts since the early twentieth century to formulate neo-Freudian theories based on eliminating repression (and indeed 'repression' has come to have negative connotations) Freud himself was clear that repression was necessary for any kind of social organization. Indeed, a world in which everyone simply obeyed the demands of the pleasure principle seems an unattractive, if not frightening, prospect.[2]

Freud (1915) distinguishes between *primal (or primary) repression*, and *secondary repression*, which he characterizes as 'repression proper'. Primal repression occurs at an early stage in the infant's development and involves the repression of ideas associated with the infant's bodily drives. This can be seen as a very early process of symbolization in which particular bodily sensations and drives, which, presumably, the small child can barely articulate, are represented as ideas. Secondary repression builds on this primary process in that ideas or images – representations, in short – that are associated with the original idea then come to be repressed in turn. Hence, the images of dreams, for example, do not necessarily mean what they seem to mean. There are chains of ideas at work, one idea symbolizing another (and another . . .). I might dream of my mother but she might in fact symbolize myself (as mother), or both of us or, indeed, my father, or my daughter, or someone or something else entirely. The meaning of the dream can only be known through its analysis, which would include the associations made by the dreamer. Its representations can signify any number of things, including images that are apparently 'opposite' ('mother' for 'father', for example), or as composites of many things ('mother' as father/daughter/self, or as simultaneously nurturer and rival). In short, dreams tell us something; as Adam Phillips has nicely put it, they are 'a way we tell ourselves secrets' (Phillips, 2005). But what they – and other 'symptoms' – tell us is by no means transparent. This is because the unconscious does not obey the logic of 'external' reality. It is not structured by time, and it is able to contain mutual contradictions, so that people or things in dreams, for example, can be more than one thing at the same time (which is how my mother could represent both herself and someone else).

---

[2] In his autobiography the poet Louis MacNeice writes, 'Freud having taught my generation that sex repression is immoral . . .', to which his editor has added the nice footnote, 'This is of course incorrect though widely believed' (MacNeice, 1982: 172).

When something is repressed, no conscious memory remains, although traces and glimpses persist since repression frequently fails – or, at least, we can only know about it when it fails. In this sense, dreams, slips of the tongue and the rest represent failed repression – in which the repressed 'returns', albeit in a disguised form. In a sense we are obliged to act it out as a means of dealing with it. However, and as I noted above, what we dream, for example, is unlikely to be a *direct* manifestation of our desires; that might be too much for our ego to bear. Instead, the unconscious uses symbols to *indicate and symbolize* those desires. So the manifest content of a dream (the things the dream is *apparently* about) does not necessarily indicate what the dream is 'actually' about. Instead, Freud argues, the twin mechanisms of *condensation* and *displacement* work to make the symbols within dreams stand for something else. Condensation occurs when a number of elements (ideas, fears, desires, etc.) are *condensed* into one image, as in, for example, composite figures which sometimes occur in dreams, or, as Minsky notes, the common dream of being naked in the middle of a city, which

> could represent the condensation of several anxieties: a generalized fear of being exposed as less confident than one might appear, anxiety about an important job interview the following day and an experience on the day before the dream of having been lost on the way to the theatre . . . (Minsky, 1996: 28–9)

Displacement occurs when one thing comes to stand for another: as in tables laid for a meal symbolizing women, for example (the fantasized provision of plenty from the mother?). In this case, the emotional energy – in psychoanalytic terms, the *cathexis* – associated with one idea or concern is displaced on to another.

Becoming human

As I noted above, the personality structure outlined by Freud is not something we are born with, neither does it spontaneously emerge. According to this framework, we become persons through a kind of forced entry into social relations of various kinds. The crisis that occurs for the child through her or his Oedipus complex – the complex around her or his love for the mother is key here. Freud's is a theory of how we *become* 'human' – how we change from savage, asocial beings (neonates) to social beings. The infant is impelled by drives (*Triebe*) – primarily, the drive towards pleasure.

Figure 5.1. Freudian developmental stages.

ORAL PHASE (*infancy*)	Pleasure derived from suckling.	PRE-OEDIPAL PERIOD
ANAL PHASE (*c. 2–3 years*)	Pleasure derived from controlling faeces.	
PHALLIC PHASE (*c. 3–4 years*)	Pleasure derived from auto-erotic genital stimulation (clitoris or penis)	OEDIPAL CRISIS
LATENCY		
GENITAL PHASE (*from puberty*)	Sexual impulses focused primarily around the vagina or the penis.	MATURE SEXUALITY

All children pass through a number of psychosexual phases, roughly corresponding to stages in their physical development (see figure 5.1). As children pass through each of these phases, their sexual energy (libido) is organized around different bodily zones. Each phase is accompanied by fantasies and desires appropriate to that stage. Sequentially, these phases are the oral, the anal and the phallic, followed by a period of sexual latency, after which the child (now an adolescent) enters the genital stage. During the oral stage, the infant takes pleasure from suckling, during the anal phase from control of her or his faeces, and during the phallic phase from masturbation of the penis or clitoris. Until the phallic phase, the child has no clear sense of self: the ego is undeveloped. As the child's self is formed, so is its gender; it is not until the phallic stage that the child becomes gendered. (She or he is, of course, assigned a gender by others: however, she or he has no clear sense of her or his own identity as a gendered being.) For Freud, gender is organized around the phallus, and children who have not yet registered the existence of the penis as something which may or not be present in a human being are ungendered. It is during and after the phallic phase that the little boy becomes *more or less* masculine and the little girl *more or less* feminine. I stress 'more or less' because, as I discuss below, at least one reading of Freudian psychoanalysis sees the achievement of gender as only an approximation. According to Jacqueline Rose, masculinity and (especially) femininity are difficult to achieve, and are only achieved incompletely. Freud's really radical insight lies in his understanding that both gender and sexuality need to be *explained*: they are not simply there at the outset. Furthermore, heterosexuality – so often taken as natural and innate – is in need of as much explanation as other forms of sexual expression. Before I consider this, however, I shall consider Freud's formulation of the Oedipal crisis in the child's psychic life.

Oedipal crises: it's different for girls

Freud began by assuming that girls and boys follow equivalent, if inverted, paths, so that the boy's first love was his mother and he experienced the father as a rival, while the girl's first love was for her father, and, for her, the mother was a rival. It was not until his 1924 paper, 'The dissolution of the Oedipus complex', that he acknowledged an asymmetry in boys' and girls' development, and not until 1925 that he began to explore the implications of this asymmetry. In three important papers – 'Some psychical consequences of the anatomical distinction between the sexes' (1925), 'Female sexuality' (1931) and 'Femininity' (1933) – he outlines his revised theory, arguing that the girl's first love, like the boy's, is for the mother, since it is she (or her substitute) who nurtures the infant.

In his revised perspective Freud argued that both boys and girls begin with an exclusive attachment to the mother, since she is the first nurturer. This persists through the oral and anal stages. During the boy's phallic stage, he begins to develop an awareness that not all humans possess a penis. This is the start of his Oedipus complex – the crisis around the boy's attachment to his mother. The boy begins to believe that those humans who do not possess a penis have been 'castrated' (as a punishment for some misdeed), and a belief that he too will be castrated if he persists in his love for his mother (thus usurping the father's place). This is the boy's castration anxiety, which leads him to repress completely his attachment to his mother. The boy gives up his mother as a love object and, as is the case with all love objects that are given up, she becomes devalued for him. The boy begins to internalize the father's law – manifest in social rules. That is, he begins to develop a strong superego. So normal masculinity involves accepting paternal authority, but (when the time comes) taking the place of that authority; and giving up the love for the mother but replacing it with the love for people like the mother (i.e. women).

The first step in the girl's phallic period is the 'momentous discovery' that some humans possess a penis, while she does not; Freud says, 'She sees it, and she knows in a flash that she does not have it and that she wants it.' This results in a sense of inadequacy, a wound to her narcissism which itself leads to an envy for the penis. Initially, the girl believes that this 'lack' is exclusive to her. When she comes to realize it is shared by all girls and women, her response, according to Freud, is to 'blame' the mother both for sharing this 'lack' and for denying the penis to the girl. Thus the strong attachment to the mother starts to weaken. But the girl's perception of lacking the penis is largely, Freud suggests, a principle around which the grievances she is beginning to feel against the mother can be organized. In other words, the turning away from the mother during the Oedipus complex is not based solely on her envy of the penis. Rather, penis envy organizes and legitimates the girl's numerous other grievances against the mother. One would, of course, expect little boys to have similar grievances against the mother. To the extent that Freud addresses this, he suggests that penis envy – the girl's impossible demand that the mother equip her with a penis – is enough to make the difference, suggesting that it both legitimates other grievances and is a grievance in itself.

According to Freud, women in analysis present a list of grievances against the mother: not only that she failed to provide a penis, but that she did not suckle her long enough, that she forced her to share the mother's love with the father and with siblings. It is important to note at this point that Freud is not implying that this is a result of faulty childcare; it is, rather, inevitable. For both boys and girls, infantile desires are incapable of satisfaction. The child is, to borrow a term from Melanie Klein, 'greedy', wanting more than she or he needs and more than it is possible to give.

The child, of course, does not know that her or his desires and demands are 'unrealistic', and a loosening (though not a breaking) of her strong ties with her mother begins. With this, the girl is ready to enter her Oedipus complex. This complex is brought about by the girl's castration anxiety (her belief that she has been castrated) – a reversal of the process in boys, for whom castration anxiety is a *consequence* of the Oedipus complex.

The girl's penis envy opens up a number of possible lines of development. She may, according to Freud, develop a 'masculinity complex', in which she refuses the idea that she does not possess a penis, or she clings to the hope of getting one. She may, instead, deny her own sexual feelings, as it were giving up hope in terms of competing with the penis. To the extent that she avoids these pitfalls (and she may not) she takes the difficult path to 'normal' femininity, in which penis envy persists in a number of ways: in the character-trait of jealousy, in a loosening of her tie with her mother and in the desire for a child. 'Normal' femininity involves giving up the wish for a penis and replacing it with the wish for a baby; (with this aim in mind) taking the father as a love object (though the tie to the mother is only loosened, not broken); the beginnings of a change of erotogenic zone, from the clitoris to the vagina; and the development of a lesser sense of justice. Because in a sense the girl cannot be 'threatened' with castration (believing herself to have already been castrated), she cannot be terrified into obeying social rules. Hence, for Freud, she has a weaker superego. I discuss this further below. The main point to note here, however, is that gender is not innate in the Freudian account: we become gendered as part of the process of becoming a (cultural) person. In becoming a person, then, we simultaneously become gendered. If we are not born gendered, it follows that we are not born with a 'sexual orientation', as we would now understand the term. After all, homosexuality, heterosexuality and even bisexuality only work if there are distinct genders in the first place. Again, I return to this issue below.

The riddle of femininity

It is worth pausing at this point to consider the issues of masculinity and femininity in the Freudian account, not least because Freud's words on women have often been taken to indicate an inherent misogyny which has, in turn, been seen as grounds for rejecting the theoretical premises of psychoanalysis. Yet the psychoanalytic take on gender has been seen as one of its most productive by many (though by no means all) feminist writers, as I discuss below. Certainly, much of the Freudian account sits uneasily with contemporary feminism. Certainly, too, many of Freud's notions, when taken out of context, can seem absurd. However, by thinking 'with and against' Freud, several writers have produced important and productive psychoanalytically informed accounts of femininity, masculinity and sexuality. The psychoanalytic account of identity is more multifaceted than it might appear.

It is useful to begin with notions of 'masculinity' and femininity' themselves. It is, I hope, clear from the sketch of development above, that masculinity and femininity are only ever approximately achieved. Furthermore, Freud was emphatic that there is no straightforward mapping of masculinity on to 'maleness' and femininity on to 'femaleness'. Masculinity is not an exclusive property of men, nor is femininity an exclusive property of women. Women are prone to masculine impulses, and vice versa. As Rowley and Gross (1992) argue, Freud sees masculinity and femininity in terms of three other sets of oppositions: active/passive, subject/object, phallic/castrated. The masculine (not male) position is aligned with the first of each of these terms, and the feminine (not female) one with the second. Yet Freud himself was not always consistent, and sometimes did conflate women with 'feminine' and men with 'masculine'. For example, in speaking of the riddle of femininity, he says,

> Nor will *you* have escaped worrying over this problem – those of you who are men; to those of you who are women this will not apply – you are yourselves the problem. (Freud, 1933: 113)

Moreover, although, as we shall see, Freud sees the path to 'normal' femininity as a difficult one that many women will not negotiate, he does seem to see adult women in terms of the characteristics he cites as 'feminine' – envious, narcissistic and so on.

Yet, within the terms of Freud's own thesis, it is strange to conceptualize women as having a weaker superego and hence a lesser sense of justice. Certainly, they cannot be terrified into obeying social rules, since, believing themselves already castrated, they cannot fear subsequent castration. On the other hand, the central place of envy in the psychic lives of girls and women ought to (and perhaps does) make them *more* attentive to social justice, as I discuss next.

Justice and envy

The issue of 'penis envy' has, of course, long been seen as a sticking point for Freudian theory; what, we might ask, is so great about the penis anyway, that the sight of it should make the little girl envy it, and that this envy should persist in the unconscious of adult women? It seems to me that there are three salient issues here. First, the little girl does not know that the penis is (over-)valued: that is not the basis of her envy. Rather, on seeing a body that is otherwise apparently identical to hers but with something more, she can be understood as fantasizing that this 'something more' is a source of satisfaction and plenitude to the boy. As Forrester notes, 'The object of envy is not what I desire, but rather what satisfies the other with whom I compare or identify myself' (1997: 24). Second, it is reasonable to point out that in this culture we *do* over-value the penis. The concept of heterosexual 'sex' is often taken to refer, not simply to genital intimacy, but specifically to penile penetration of the vagina. It is not unknown, either, to come across the view that women can't have 'sex' with other women, the absence of any penis at all seemingly making 'sex' impossible. In the popular imaginary, sex seems very often to hinge on the presence of the penis. And not only must this penis exist, it should be capable of becoming hard (witness the sales of Viagra) and it should also, pre-sumably, be large. Every day I receive emails inviting me to increase the size and girth of 'my' penis, and presumably these messages are speaking to some cultural anxiety. (It is true that these emails are often phrased in terms of the benefits to a female partner. But it doesn't seem far-fetched to suggest that if the desired result were really only about women's sexual pleasure, there might be easier and more straightforward ways for heterosexual men to achieve this than enlarg-ing their penises.) Little boys seem to be given more names for their genitals than are little girls, and those names seem to be more socially acceptable. This valorizing of the penis is also institutionally sup-ported in that it is enshrined in law. For example, legal marriage in the United Kingdom requires a speech act ('I do' etc.) followed by a sex act. This sex act must be penile penetration of the vagina. And the crime of rape requires the active presence of a penis. It is not only in the pages of psychoanalytic studies that the penis is understood as having a significance beyond itself.

Third, envy has something of a bad press, and it is after all one of the seven deadly sins of the Christian tradition. But it is not itself much of a problem in psychoanalytic schemata. As Frosh puts it,

> Given Melanie Klein's revelations of the degree of envy existing in every individual subject, male or female, a little bit more or less, attached or not, does not seem likely to make much difference. (Frosh, 1997: 177–8)

Klein, like Freud, emphasizes the discontent of the child's inner world, and emphasizes, too, the argument that it is impossible for the mother to fulfil the child's wants. The child has a relentless and overwhelming desire – to be loved exclusively, never to want or wait for anything, to wholly own the mother, to be at the centre of the uni-verse – and part of the process of becoming human involves bearing the knowledge that such desires cannot be fulfilled (Klein, 1932, 1962). For both Freud and Klein envy is inevitable; it is not a moral failing. In both their analyses, envy is related to what is believed to satisfy the mother: that to which the mother can claim a right and which is denied to the child (this may or may not be an actual 'father'). The point is that something is denied – and must be denied – to the child, and this provokes her or his envy.

Further, and as John Forrester has argued, from a psychoanalytic perspective envy is crucial in the social world. It underpins our sense of, and our desires for, justice. For Freud, envy is central to our sense of justice; as Forrester notes, 'without envy, not only would there be no *need* for a judicial apparatus, there would be no *desire* for justice' (Forrester, 1997: 20, emphasis in original). In other words, our sense of fairness stems from envy – usually regarded as a baser emotion than the high ideals of justice would suggest. The expression 'the politics of envy' is often used as a code for a kind of grubby, second-rate politics, based on self-interest. For Freud, however, the whole politics of social justice is built on unconscious envy. *We do without things so that other people will also have to do without them.* As Forrester puts it, 'The high ideal of social justice tendentiously cloaks something altogether more individually self-interested' (1997: 16). If I can't have something, you certainly won't have it either. Thus is justice born.

As I noted above, this insight suggests, of course, that women ought to have a *stronger* sense of justice than men, since they are more prone to envy. That Freud does not appear to have noticed this would seem to indicate something of a blind spot with regard to women. Similarly, his notion that mature female sexuality involves a concentration of sensation on the vagina, and away from the clitoris, tells us more about the preconceptions of his time than about women themselves. Indeed, many writers have taken it as axiomatic that Freudian theory is fundamentally misogynist, based on a model of women and girls as 'lacking'. It is true that women and girls tend to be bit-part players in the high Freudian drama between fathers and sons. Yet this same drama offers some intriguing and productive insights on the ways in which gender and sexuality are produced. It also offers a way of seeing beyond what is apparent on the surface to consider the difficulties of being and becoming gendered and sexed human beings. As such, it confounds a commonplace view of both gender and sexuality as innate and essential. This is why, as the next section discusses in more detail, psychoanalytic perspectives have been taken up with enthusiasm by some strands of feminism.

Psychoanalysis and feminism

It is worth briefly tracing the history of this development through (an also brief) consideration of two texts which are undoubtedly now dated but which proved pivotal in the take-up of Freud within feminist and other analyses of gender and sexuality. These texts are Nancy Chodorow's *The Reproduction of Mothering* (first published in 1970) and Juliet Mitchell's *Psychoanalysis and Feminism* (first published in 1974). Both Chodorow and Mitchell have, in different ways and to differing degrees, moved away from the positions presented in the two texts, so this outline is not intended to situate these writers' positions, but rather to show something of a turning point in both feminist and psychoanalytic theorizing.

The two works, while both drawing on psychoanalysis, take entirely different positions, although both, as I shall argue, suffer from similar problems. Chodorow, like a number of other feminist writers, rejected the Freudian schema in favour of an object relations account which emphasizes the child's early (pre-Oedipal) relationship with the mother. Within such accounts the self is understood as developing primarily through relations with others, rather than through the 'drives' of Freud's theoretical schema. The mother assumes a more central place in the formation of this self. Chodorow attempted to achieve a psychosocial analysis in her argument that women – largely as compensation for men's failure to nurture them – make heavy emotional and psychic investments in desiring and nurturing children. Ultimately, masculine and feminine personality structures are presented by Chodorow as the outcome of the ways in which children are mothered and fathered: and of course that very mothering and fathering is an outcome of the masculine and feminine personality structure produced in the parents' own childhood. The result is that women mother daughters who value connection, and so want to be mothers in turn, while men unconsciously fear and devalue connectedness, leaving their heterosexual partners uncared for, and so on.

In *Psychoanalysis and Feminism*, Mitchell sought to put psychoanalysis at the service of a feminist project by considering unconscious attachments to, and investments in, systems of gender and sexuality. In this she was writing directly against the orthodoxy of the time, which was to see psychoanalysis as fundamentally antithetical to any notion of feminism and indeed as deeply misogynist, as well as being politically reactionary. She was also attempting to find ways of theorizing (gender) inequality outside an orthodox Marxist analysis that seemed to her unable to account for inequalities other than those of class (Mitchell, 1995).

Mitchell sought to rescue the Freudian account from biological reductionism by reading Freud through the French psychoanalyst Jacques Lacan,[3] using his perspective to argue that culture is organized around male authority. This is not in itself a very contentious claim, but

[3] I do not have space here to discuss Lacan's perspective, but it is worth noting that he saw his work as a 'return' to what was truly radical in Freud. His work stresses cultural and linguistic aspects of sexual difference, and has thus been seen by some as preferable to the biologism of Freud's account.

Mitchell also argues that psychoanalysis gives us the tools to see, for example, how women internalize a culture that is oppressive to them – how we do not always act in our own self-interests. The key point, for Mitchell, is that psychoanalysis does not offer a *prescription for* a (patriarchal) society: it does not claim that women *ought to* become feminine or that men *ought to* become masculine, still less that women ought to be subordinate to men. Rather, it offers a *description of* a (patriarchal) society, showing how women become feminine and men masculine, because of the demands of the culture, rather than because of any innate masculinity or femininity.

There is no doubt that *Psychoanalysis and Feminism* did a great deal to reconceptualize Freudian psychoanalysis, even if many – perhaps most – feminists were not won over by its arguments. *The Reproduction of Mothering* enjoyed massive influence, especially in the United States, where, as Doane and Hodges (1992) argue, its influence was 'almost hegemonic' among feminist theorists. There are several problems with both analyses but I want to focus here on those which centre on the relationship between the unconscious and social relations. To do this I shall outline the critique made from within psychoanalysis by Jacqueline Rose.

Like Mitchell, though unlike Chodorow, Rose takes a broadly Lacanian approach to the question of gender, but reaches different conclusions from both. Rose (1987) argues that the question of whether psychoanalysis is a description of, or a prescription for, a male-dominated society is simply the wrong question. While Mitchell used psychoanalysis to explain why, for example, women adapt to 'feminine' roles (when it may well be against their objective interests to do so), and Chodorow explains gendered personality structures as the outcome of gendered social roles, Rose argues that in fact what psychoanalysis can show us is that women (and men) *do not* adapt to such roles, or at least do not necessarily adapt to them, do not necessarily internalize the norms of the social world. For her, the 'fundamental premise' of this work is the assumption that women and men really do internalize the norms of gender. While accepting that psychoanalysis is not entirely satisfactory, Rose argues that its force is to show precisely that the norms *do not work*: in this, it shows that 'something is being forced'. In turn, this reveals the norms themselves as something other than 'natural' and innate. For Rose, 'the basic premise and indeed starting point of psychoanalysis' is that the internalization of norms does not work:

The unconscious constantly reveals the 'failure' of identity. Because there is no continuity of psychic life, so there is no stability of sexual identity, no position for women (or for men) which is ever simply achieved. Nor does psychoanalysis see such 'failure' as a special-case inability or an individual deviancy from the norm. 'Failure' is not a moment to be regretted in a process of adaptation, or development into normality . . . Instead 'failure' is something endlessly repeated and relived moment by moment throughout our individual histories. It appears not only in the symptom, but also in dreams, in slips of the tongue and in forms of sexual pleasure that are pushed to the sidelines of the norm. (Rose, 1987: 187)

She argues that psychoanalysis's recognition of the failure of identity is part of its value:

[P]sychoanalysis becomes one of the few places in our culture where it is recognized as more than a fact of individual pathology that most women do not painlessly slip into their roles as women, if indeed they do at all. (Rose, 1987: 184)

We should of course add that men do not 'painlessly slip into their roles' either, and that masculinity, as well as femininity, is precarious. However, femininity for Freud (and for Lacan and Rose) is particularly difficult, since, as we saw earlier, 'normal' heterosexual femininity involves both a change of erotogenic zone and a change to the gender of the love object. Rose's reading of Freud stresses the paradoxical normality of a failure properly to achieve (socially) normal femininity. The process of becoming feminine is a process involving injury: it is not that femininity *is* injury, as many commentators have assumed; it is, rather, that injury is the *price* of becoming feminine (Rose, 1987).

This issue of failure is an important one. Rather than characterizing a specific group of (other) people as 'perverts' or 'hysterics' or 'unadapted', psychoanalysis locates such 'failures' within all of us, which is why neurosis is itself normal. Repression may be necessary, but, as Freud pointed out and as Rose reminds us, the civilizing process has its costs. More fundamentally, perhaps, and as I pointed out earlier, Freud takes masculinity/femininity and heterosexuality as *phenomena to be explained*, rather than as 'givens'. In this respect psychoanalysis has been taken up by (some) feminists as a means of explaining how we achieve the identities 'men' or 'women'. Such identities, from this perspective, are only achieved approximately and with difficulty. Further, they are never achieved once and for all but are the product of ongoing unconscious (as well as conscious) activity. This emphasis on contingency and fluidity means that, from this perspective, one can never, once and for all, 'be' masculine or femi-nine, or (as conventionally understood) heterosexual or homosexual. Rather, we must unconsciously deal with multiple forms of desire, identification and anxiety. To give just one, brief, example: Freud (1922), in discussing 'normal' jealousy, discusses the possibility that

> A man will not only feel pain about the woman he loves and hatred of the man who is his rival, but also grief about the man, whom he loves uncon-sciously, and hatred of the woman as his rival; and this latter set of feel-ings will add to the intensity of his feelings. (Freud, 1922: 223)

Desires, then, may be more diverse than we consciously allow. And so may identifications. Freud adds,

> I even know of a man who suffered extraordinarily during his attacks of jealousy and who, according to his own account, went through unen-durable torments by consciously imagining himself in the position of the faithless woman. (Freud, 1922: 223)

As we shall see in the next chapter, such an emphasis on polymor-phous desire and multiple identifications forms the basis of Judith Butler's analysis of gender as doing, rather than being.

I have, in this chapter, concentrated on identities of sex and sexual-ity, and it is fair to say that these identities have been at the centre of much of the psychoanalytic gaze. Indeed, in classical psychoanalysis, sexual desire has been seen as underwriting all aspects of human behaviour – even if they appeared to be something else, so that what might look like (for example) racism or class antagonism must always be *really* about sexual desire. However, it is important to stress that there is a considerable psychoanalytic literature which analyses iden-tities of 'race' and nation, and, to a lesser extent, those of social class. This work is important in situating psychic processes within wider social relations which are cross-cut by relations of inequality. As Carolyn Steedman has eloquently argued,

> Freud's re-writing of the myth of Oedipus is a highly specific account, centred on the particularity of losing a parent as a possession, of the loss that it is the fate of every human child to suffer in some way or other. If there were no history, if people were not conscious of themselves living within time and society, and if they did not use their own past to construct explanations of the present, then the myth – this particular one, others like it – could be allowed to stand, as a timeless and universal allegory of human development. But we live in time and politics, and exclusion is the promoter of envy, the social and subjective sense of the impossible unfairness of things. The first loss, the first exclusion, will be differently

interpreted by the adult who used to be the child, according to the social circumstances she finds herself in, and the story she needs to relate. (Steedman, 1986: 111)

I do not have space here adequately to explore the rich and complex psychoanalytic literature on 'race', nation and class, but I do want to make the point that all of this literature provides ways of conceptualizing social identities through considering aspects of personhood that are not necessarily apparent, but which nevertheless can be seen as structuring our selves and our relations with others. In the context of a Western emphasis on 'reason', all that is 'irrational', 'wild and 'savage' can be disavowed. As such, we can imagine ourselves safe from it. But disavowal does not make those non-rational feelings go away. Indeed, they can be seen as ubiquitous in the social world. Political appeals of all kinds are frequently mobilized, not on the basis of 'reason', but by playing on fears, desires and dreads. The entire rhetoric of the far-right British National Party, for example, centres on the agitation of fears that 'they' have taken things that are denied to 'us'. 'Foreigners' get decent housing, government handouts and so on, while the indigenous population (for which read, in BNP rhetoric, the indigenous *white* population) is ignored. This is surely about more than a rational means–end calculation and involves, at least in part, deep-seated fears, desires and envies. More generally, think of the horror provoked by certain kinds of identities: the kind of horror that provokes the response, 'I would rather die than be like that!' (Butler, 1993). Or the ways in which certain groups come to be associated with dirt, disease and pollution. Psychoanalysis forces us to ask hard questions about such reactions and responses, not simply in terms of individual pathology, but in terms of structured patterns of social relationships that give rise to particular kinds of psychic engagement.

Concluding remarks

I have argued throughout this chapter that psychoanalysis gives us various means of understanding non-rational, concealed aspects of identity. It posits a model of identity in which the unconscious has a central place and in which we can only know ourselves incompletely and with some difficulty. Is it a useful model for a sociology of identity? I hope that I have indicated in this chapter some of the ways in which relations of inequality can be seen as structuring our 'inner world' in very fundamental ways.

Psychoanalytic perspectives give us various tools for theorizing identity that are absent from other accounts and that enable us to see an alliance between 'personal' and 'social', albeit an uneasy one. Although, as I have been arguing throughout, identity and personhood are produced within the social world rather than being somehow 'outside' or 'beyond' or 'prior to' the social, it is important to recognize that people are not simply cultural or social dupes, slotting neatly into assigned roles and places. The social world is messier than this and part of the messiness, it seems to me, derives from the messiness of the unconscious.

None of this is to deny the problems of psychoanalytic accounts – their ambiguous relationships to gender and sexuality, for example, or their overwhelming emphasis on the (heterosexual) family. But in the end, following Frosh, I should like to be both 'for and against psychoanalysis': against an unquestioning orthodoxy, and against the authoritarian moralizing of some of its forms, but for its marvellous and relentless hermeneutics of suspicion that mistrusts the apparent and looks instead for different sets of meanings. Frosh argues,

> [W]hat I want to advocate is an intense and, if possible, ambivalent engagement with the psychoanalytic project of mapping the unconscious, of articulating a new rationality which is based on *reason* (and so is not mystical) but which is also respectful of emotion and irrationality – 'unreason' – and which does not close its eyes in the dark. (Frosh, 1997: 231, emphasis in original)

6 Masquerading as ourselves: self-impersonation and social life

Introduction: between semblance and substance

People in the West conventionally counterpose *being* an (authentic) identity against *doing* an identity (performing). While the former is assumed to be an expression of 'who we are, really', the latter is usually assumed to be playing a part: a 'false' expression, denying, negating or concealing 'who we are really'. When contestants leave the 'Big Brother' house, for example, they often claim that the *other* contestants were 'acting' or 'wearing masks', while they, on the contrary, were always 'being themselves'. The distinction rests on an assumption that it is possible – and indeed desirable – for one's 'true self' simply to emerge. When a gap is seen to exist between doing and being – or semblance and substance – then the person is liable to be accused of pretension, inauthenticity or 'acting a role'. It is taken, therefore, that semblance and substance ought to coincide. If semblance does not match substance, that is because of some dissembling – some attempt to deceive others, perhaps to make them believe that we are nicer/more interesting/more virtuous than we 'really are'.

Certainly, it is acknowledged that most of us will don 'masks' at certain points – perhaps from self-preservation – but there is assumed to a real person 'behind' the mask. In most cases, this 'real person' is assumed to be more authentic then the 'mask' or 'masquerade'. To be 'acting' is understood to be acting inauthentically. Alison Young describes semblance and substance as 'two orders of being' that (it is assumed) need to be kept distinct. When they are not kept distinct, she argues, there is a 'misidentification of appearance and reality' (Young,

1996: 112). Reality, of course, is seen to inhere in substance (who we are really) rather than in semblance (who we appear to be). Concerns around such a gap were rather brutally exploited by tabloid press reportage of what became known as 'the Bulger case' in the United Kingdom in 1993. In this case, two 10-year-old boys found guilty of murdering a toddler, James Bulger, were depicted as 'fiends' whose 'evil' nature was masked by their *appearance* as 'normal' schoolboys (an appearance reinforced by the school-photograph-type snapshots of those boys which were used by the media).

Young argues that reportage presents the boys in the following terms.

> They *appear* to be children but are not: they are more like evil adults or monsters in disguise. Evil is the lack of correspondence between appearance and being: Thompson and Venables [the killers] *appear* to be children but *are not*. James Bulger, on the other hand, *appears* child-*like* and is the quintessence of childhood. His innocence consists in the absolute correspondence between his image and his substance. (Young, 1996: 115, emphasis in original)

This grim example centres on one manifestation of a much broader social and cultural preoccupation with authenticity. It is a troubling issue when there is deemed to be a gap between semblance and substance. The trouble itself centres on anxieties about authenticity. Yet ways of resolving this 'trouble' are not straightforward. Certainly there is a belief that the outer form *ought* to express the 'inner self', but there are examples throughout Western culture (and beyond) of occasions where the outer form is represented as *less* attractive than the inner self.

A classic example occurs in folk stories: Cinderella, for example, has her noble birth disguised by being forced to act as a servant and to wear rough, servant's clothing. Yet justice magically prevails as her mother's grave or her fairy godmother (depending on the version) yields clothes suitable for the social position of her birth. Eventually, of course, Cinderella marries the prince because she is the only woman whose foot fits the tiny shoe she has left at the ball (tiny feet, across many cultures, signifying high-class femininity). So Cinderella is 'really' of aristocratic lineage, but her transformation into her 'real self' can only be achieved when semblance matches substance and she is transformed into *looking like* a princess. Cinderella's story disrupts the conventional wisdom that the 'surface' is suspect. In changing her surface appearance, she becomes who she really is.

In contemporary popular culture, the Cinderella theme is continued in television series such as *The Swan* (in the United States) and

Ten Years Younger (in the United Kingdom), with the place of the mother or fairy godmother being taken by a series of experts – a 'personal stylist', a make-up artist, a cosmetic surgeon, a dentist and a hairdresser. The format of the Channel 4 series, *Ten Years Younger*, for example, is as follows: a middle-aged woman is taken around a town centre, while onlooking members of the public are invited to guess her age. Inevitably, they overestimate her age. The woman is then given a 'makeover', involving cosmetic surgery and new clothes, hairstyle and make-up. The first stage is then repeated: members of the public are again invited to guess her age. This time, and just as inevitably, they underestimate it, to the thrilled response of the woman herself and the 'expert' who has taken her in hand.

As Gillian Bennett (2005) points out, the woman has of course been made over not once but twice – once 'downwards' (harsh lighting, no make-up, bad clothes) and once 'upwards', to heighten the before-and-after transformative contrast. But what is perhaps most interesting is the way in which, after the transformation, the woman's 'outside' is presented as at last properly matching her 'inside':

> Miraculously, the outside now corresponded to the inside where, we were led to believe, a younger, trendier – though up to now invisible – person had always been hiding. . . [N]ow Plain Jane has become Beautiful Barbie, she can fulfil her potential and let her true self emerge from the shadows. (Bennett, 2005: 29)

In other words, the woman becomes who she 'really' is by changing the 'exterior' manifestation of her self. This is one manifestation of an old and widespread theme, which might appear to be paradoxical – that is, using a mask (in this case the Botox, the hairstyle, the new clothes) to show who you *really* are.

Persons, selves and masks

Wendy Doniger argues that

> We assume that masquerades lie, and often they do, at least on the surface. But often masquerades tell a deeper truth, that masquerading as ourselves reaffirms an enduring self (or network of selves) inside us, which does not change even if our masquerades, intentional or helpless, make us look different to others. (Doniger, 2005: 203)

Self-impersonation is a concept I owe to Doniger, and I shall use it throughout the rest of this chapter. While we are accustomed to understanding 'impersonation' as meaning fraudulently or otherwise assuming the characteristics of *another person*, I am using it here to mean a process by which we assume characteristics we claim as our own. Through this process, we become (social) persons through performing our selves. From this perspective, asking who is behind the mask, or investigating the gap between semblance and substance, is not the issue. Rather, what we need to consider is what underwrites a contemporary concern with 'authenticity' in the first place. Not, then, how we can be authentic, but what we mean by authentic, why it is desirable, and what follows from a splitting of behaviours, acts and identities into 'authentic' and 'inauthentic'.

In this emphasis, I am drawing on the work of two social theorists whose work comes from two quite different positions. Erving Goffman (1922–82) was a Canadian sociologist whose work is linked with a symbolic interactionist tradition (even as it transcends symbolic interactionism). The North American feminist philosopher Judith Butler (b. 1956) draws far more explicitly on a European tradition of philosophical inquiry; her influences include Hegel, Freud and Lacan, Foucault, Derrida and Austin (see Salih, 2002). Her work is associated with Queer Theory – a term which refers to a range of perspectives that seek to destabilize the notion of a coherent, unified and stable sexual identity. There are fundamental and important differences between Goffman and Butler, and I discuss these further below. I have found thinking about the differences between them important and provocative in thinking about identity. Nevertheless, they also have important things in common. For both, identity is *always* something that is done: it is achieved, rather than innate. However, identity is not something achieved in isolation; it is part of a social and collective endeavour, not an individual odyssey. Further, it is not a matter of individual 'choice': I cannot simply choose to be one person rather than another (although I may resist the positioning of others). The question, then, is not 'who we are really' but how we achieve identity, under what constraints and in what contexts. These constraints and contexts matter: while both theorists, and perhaps Goffman in particular, have been characterized as emphasizing freedom, agency and the 'micro' world of interaction, it is clear that both see individual actions and responses as part of a wider social order that permits some actions and disallows others.

Dramas and lives

Goffman is perhaps best known for his dramaturgic metaphor, in which social interaction and social identity are analysed by reference to theatrical performances. Butler, similarly, is concerned to analyse how we 'do' identities (and she is primarily concerned with gendered identities) through performance. Language, however, fails us in both cases, since 'performance' tends to indicate the adoption of a character more or less at will and, further, the adoption of a character that neither we nor others take to be our own. It is a different thing, after all (even if it were possible), for me to 'be' 'Gertrude' in *Hamlet* than for me to be (the character I and others recognize as) 'Stephanie Lawler'. So it is important to be clear at the outset that neither Goffman nor Butler envisages 'performance' in this way. Nevertheless, it is a useful concept with which to think identity, even if it can lead to misunderstandings.

Goffman's use of the idea of 'regions' in which the self is performed is the source of one such misunderstanding. Goffman argues that in life, as in the theatre, there are 'front stage' and 'backstage' regions. In the front stage regions, we are aware of our audience and in a sense we play to them. Goffman himself uses the example of someone waiting on tables whose every aspect of behaviour is different in the dining room (front stage) from in the kitchen (backstage). Another example is the lecturer who more or less consciously performs 'lecturer' while giving a lecture, but then behaves differently over lunch with friends, and perhaps differently again when alone.

It is sometimes assumed that this therefore means that we are truly 'ourselves' – that we slip the mask – when backstage. Doniger, for example, argues (disapprovingly) that

> Erving Goffman speaks of 'the field of public life' wherein our public self must play its part, versus a 'backstage' where the individual can relax before having to put on the theatrical persona; only when we are alone can we take off the mask. Goffman assumes that the private self is unmasked, that we are most genuinely ourselves when alone. (Doniger, 2005: 203–4)

But while Goffman is ambiguous, I disagree with Doniger that he represents the 'backstage' self as 'unmasked' or more 'real'. There are two reasons why I argue this: first, his view of persons and roles, and second, his view of 'role distance'. I outline both next.

Mask, masquerade and character

Goffman points out that the original use of the word 'person' derives from *persona* – the masks worn by characters in Greek tragedies. In other words, to be a person is to be a mask – to play a role. As Doniger notes, 'The word means "that through [*per*] which the sound [of the actor's voice, *sona*] is heard". That is, the actor's presence was an integral part of the mask; he animated it, and it animated him' (Doniger, 2005: 203).

Goffman quotes Park, who writes,

> It is probably no mere historical accident that the word person, in its first meaning, is a mask. It is rather a recognition of the fact that everyone is always and everywhere, more or less consciously, playing a role . . . It is in these roles that we know each other; it is in these roles that we know ourselves. (Park, 1950: 249, quoted in Goffman, 1990: 30)

And

> In a sense, and in so far as this mask represents the conception we have formed of ourselves – the role we are striving to live up to – this mask is our truer self, the self we would like to be. In the end, our conception of our role becomes second nature and an integral part of our personality. We come into the world as individuals, achieve character, and become persons. (Park, 1950: 250, quoted in Goffman, 1990: 30)

Goffman here is arguing for something much more profound than the idea that we play roles: he is arguing that roles, or performances, far from masking the 'true person' (as is commonly assumed) are what *make us persons*. As Hacking comments,

> Throughout Goffman's work the idea of *role* is central. But it is not that of an essential person who plays various roles. The roles are not gliding surfaces that conceal the true person. The roles become aspects of the person, some more owned, some more resented, but always an evolving side of what the person is. (Hacking, 2004: 290)

What this suggests is that there is no meaningful sense in which there is a doer behind the deed, or a person behind the mask. We are, as Lemert (1997) comments, copying an imagined original; knowing, more or less consciously, the repertoire of behaviours associated with our roles, we do those behaviours over and over again: they become second nature. We are constantly playing various parts, but what those parts add up to is *ourselves*.

To be a person, then, is to perform being a person. Occasionally, especially in new situations, we might be conscious of this, but mostly we are not. Goffman nevertheless argues that we are continuously doing our various, shifting and possibly contradictory roles. Further, there are many ways in which we try to make the invisible visible in order to dramatize our roles. Put simply, it's no good doing (or being) something if no one recognizes that we are doing (or being) it. So, we need to spend energy not only on action but also on making that action apparent. For Goffman this is *dramatic realization,* and it rests on impression management. The student being ostentatiously attentive (or bored), the person sighing and looking at their watch as they wait for a late-arriving friend, the mother who pulls an exasperated face as her child misbehaves – all of these are engaging in dramatic realization. This is not to say that they are being fraudulent in any meaningful sense. Rather, it indicates that much of what we do, consciously or not, is done for the benefit of the social group of which we are a part – whether or not there is anyone actually there to witness us. Perhaps this is most obvious when it fails, when people are not recognized in ways in which they want or expect to be recognized.

As Goffman points out, we are accustomed to distinguishing between 'true' and 'false' performances, but, he argues, that is not where the line should be drawn. The distinction, rather, should be between convincing and unconvincing performances: between those that 'work' and those that do not. If this sounds overly cynical, it is important to stress that Goffman is not suggesting that (confidence tricksters aside) people are consciously manipulating or tricking one another. Rather, he suggests, all social life is artificial; it is just that we bracket off some aspects as 'real' or 'true' and others as unreal and untrue. Further, the 'performing' of identity is an *inevitable* process and, indeed, we could hardly be a part of the social world without it. As Ann Branaman observes, for Goffman

> The self is a social product in two senses. First, it is a product of the performances that individuals put on in social situations. There is no essence that exists inside an individual, waiting to be given expression in social situations. Rather, the sense of self arises as a result of publicly validated performances. Yet, secondly, even though individuals play an active role in fashioning these self-indicating performances, they are generally constrained to present images of themselves that can be socially supported in the context of a given status hierarchy. Thus, the self is a social product in the sense that it depends upon validation awarded and withheld in accordance with the norms of a stratified society. (Branaman, 1997: xlvi)

The self, then, does not *cause* a social situation; it occurs as a *result* of social situations:

> The self, then, as a performed character, is not an organic thing that has a specific location, whose fundamental fate is to be born, to mature, and to die; it is a dramatic effect arising diffusely from a scene that is presented, and the characteristic issue, the crucial concern, is whether it will be credited or discredited. (Goffman, 1990: 245)

Social identity, and indeed social reality, are made through performance.

The sacred and the profane

So far, I have outlined Goffman's dramaturgic metaphor and its implications for an analysis of the person. I hope it is clear from this that the person, for Goffman, is not *behind* the mask; rather, it *is* the mask. While he does sometimes suggest a rather underdeveloped (and unsocialized) form of self lurking behind or outside the performance, he is also explicit that, while there are occasions on which we are more or less relaxed, and while we tend to behave differently in different settings, this does not mean that we are 'ourselves' in some settings and 'acting' in others. Goffman considers this belief to be an example of a distinction between the 'sacred' (in this context, pure, untainted by the social, true) and the 'profane' (tainted by the social, less true). He challenges what he sees as the 'vulgar tendency in social thought' (Goffman, 1961: 41) to see the sacred as the self which is away from the interaction (the self with one's lover, or by oneself, for example) and the profane as that self 'exacted by society' and obedient to social rules. Instead, he suggests that there is no self which is untouched by or is outside the social world.

Perhaps we can see this most clearly in the concept of role distance. When we distance ourselves from our social roles we are inviting our audience to see us as we (would like them to think we) 'really' are – as when politicians appear on television in casual clothes to emphasize that they are not *only* politicians, and indeed are very like 'you and me'. In this they are engaging in role distance, apologizing, in Goffman's terms, for their entire role. There is an attempt to convince us that we are seeing a more authentic self – an effect also attained, or at least hoped for, when public figures seem to pause to search for words. The writer Alan Bennett – like Goffman an acute observer of everyday life – commenting on the Queen's speech following the death of Diana, Princess of Wales, notes that the Queen seemed inauthentic.

> HMQ [Her Majesty the Queen] gives an unconvincing broadcast [following the death of Diana, Princess of Wales]: 'unconvincing' not because one doesn't believe her sentiments are genuine (as to that there's no way of telling), but because she's not a good actress, indeed not an actress at all. What she should have been directed to do is to throw in a few pauses and seem to be searching for her words, then the speech would have been hailed as moving and heartfelt. As it is she reels her message off, as she

always does. That is the difference between Princess Diana and the Queen: one could act, the other can't. (Bennett, 2005: 215–16)

The pausing, stammering and hesitating public figure is displaying no more and no less authenticity than her or his counterpart who reads from a script. The performance of role distance is exactly that – another performance.

Role distance is just one example of the ways in which people play multiple roles. Goffman's great insight here is not simply to challenge us to question the dividing line between 'false' and 'authentic', not simply to show how the self escapes and exceeds its roles, not simply to show us that the self is a social product, but to show in detail how we as social actors daily participate in the constitution of such a self and, in the process, make and remake the social every day through our social interaction.

It is possible to see that people do behave in relatively regularized ways, that they develop habits which are relatively idiosyncratic as well as obeying social rules and social 'custom and practice'. If they did not, we would hardly be able to describe someone's actions as 'out of character'. Does this, then, indicate that there really is an essential person behind the mask – underneath it all, as it were?

Ian Hacking argues that Goffman, like Michel Foucault, eschews the concept of 'human nature' within his theoretical framework. But, again like Foucault, he is concerned with what it is to be a human character in the absence of 'human nature'. Both Goffman and Foucault address 'questions of how some of a person's possibilities grow into their very being, while others are excluded. This is the question of the dynamics of human nature' (Hacking, 2004: 288). 'The dynamics of human nature' is a phrase that suggests a 'human nature' that is produced through creativity and change, and indeed this is exactly how Hacking characterizes both Foucault's and Goffman's perspectives on 'human nature'. For Goffman, as already noted, we achieve character through becoming persons – that is, through our performance of a repertoire of parts. Performances occur within social milieux that determine what role can and cannot be taken, how it can be performed, and so on. This echoes Judith Butler's comment that we improvise within scenes of constraint (Butler, 2004a: 2). If character is the 'us-ness' of us – if it is the thing that (is considered to) make us what we are, then it is effectively our 'essence'.

Yet this 'character', for Goffman at least, is not something with which we are born. Remember, he argues that we achieve character through becoming persons. So character is something we attain in our performance of parts – in our self-imitation. In the quotidian detail of life, in the large and (more usually) small choices that we make, we become who we are (see Hacking, 2004).

This is a perspective that cuts through an essentialism/ constructionism binarism – a binarism that can become sterile. For Goffman, as Hacking suggests, human essence is not (as is now commonly assumed) in our genes, nor is it in some idea of a 'soul'. Indeed, it is not innate in any way. Rather, it is dynamically and temporally *done*.[1] There is a continuity of character, but it is not innate or 'natural': it is achieved through series on series of performances. And these performances are fundamentally and intrinsically social. We are tied to the 'character' of such performances by a range of factors, of which social locations of various kinds are decisive. But it is in the improvisations that we exercise moral choice, and this choice is important in the creation and maintenance of an ethical subjectivity. Again, this ethical sense is not innate but is produced through layer upon layer of performance. Like identity itself, it becomes itself through the process of being done.

> Universal human nature is not a very human thing. By acquiring it, the person becomes a kind of construct, built up not from inner psychic properties but from moral rules that are impressed on him from without . . . The general capacity to be bound by moral rules may well belong to the individual, but the particular set of rules which transforms him [*sic*] into a human being derives from requirements established in the ritual organization of social encounters. (Goffman, 1967: 45)

The interaction order

It is important to note the very social character of this interaction. Goffman is concerned with the details of everyday life, but it is far from the case that he is unconcerned with large-scale social rules. Indeed, for Goffman, the quotidian details of life are small-scale demonstrations of these 'big' social rules. It would be unwise to overstate the case, but it is clear that an emphasis on the sacred, ritualized nature of the social world characterizes at least some of his work. For Goffman (here very clearly following Emile Durkheim) interaction

---

[1] In this of course there are similarities, as Hacking (2004) notes, with the existentialist mantra 'existence precedes essence'. There is not space here adequately to explore existentialism so I simply note this point.

is a ritual and has meaning well beyond the individuals involved. Interactions are 'sacred' in the sense that, like religious ceremonies, they give us a sense of our social belonging and our sacredness as persons. Involvement in interaction (eye contact, smiling, nodding, frowning, etc.) is an act of social worship and social binding. To disrupt the interaction is to disrupt society:

> To the degree that a performance highlights the common official values of the society in which it occurs, we may look on it, in the manner of Durkheim and Radcliffe-Brown, as a ceremony – as an expressive rejuvenation and reaffirmation of the moral values of the community. Furthermore, in so far as the expressive bias of performances comes to be accepted as reality, then that which is accepted at the moment as reality will have some of the characteristics of a celebration. To stay in one's room away from the place where the party is being given . . . is to stay away from where reality is being performed. The world, in truth, is a wedding. (Goffman, 1990: 45)

Goffman suggests that this is not something we have much of a choice over, since the social order is built on particular rules of behaving and performing – this is what he calls the interaction order. Can we break these rules? Obviously in principle we can, but then others will often try to cover for us. If someone acts completely out of an acceptable frame – if, for example, they shout when silence is expected, or dance when stillness is required, others may try to make it a joke, or to pretend that nothing untoward is happening. When this is impossible – when the performance is so far from what we expect in a given situation, then we are often nervous, horrified or embarrassed. Furthermore, we feel the horror and embarrassment in our bodies – a clear indication that the social world is deeply incorporated.

Of course, the specifics of space and place are important here. They constitute the *frame* of the interaction. The concept of 'frame' is important for Goffman. Frames define the setting, organizing experience into meaningful frameworks (Goffman, 1974). People frame, however, not at random or out of personal preference, but on the basis of what is more generally framed within their specific social context. We understand what is going on because it (or something very like it) is part of our social world.

One kind of framing device occurs around gender. In this context, framing confers a *significance* on any differences that exist between men and women. There is, for example, and as he notes, no *intrinsic* reason why men and women should be assigned different (public) toilets. The 'work' done by this gender segregation, however, is to entrench gendered differences so that people learn at a very early age how to frame themselves and others within such a context:

> Every physical surround, every room, every box for social gatherings, necessarily provides materials that can be used in the display of gender and the affirmation of gender identity. (Goffman, 1977: 324)

In his work on gender relations Goffman argues that the profoundly social character of gendered norms and gendered arrangements is concealed from us by 'the doctrine of natural expression', a doctrine that 'teaches us that expressions occur because it is only natural for them to do so – no other reason being required' (Goffman, 1979: 8). Against this Goffman argues that the performative enactment of masculinity and femininity does not simply *express* gender difference, but *constitutes it*. It is (in the Durkheimian sense) a political ceremony, affirming each sex's place in the social world:

> What the human nature of males and females really consists of, then, is a capacity to learn to provide and to read depictions of masculinity and femininity and a willingness to adhere to a schedule for presenting these pictures, and this capacity they have by virtue of being persons, not females or males. One might just as well say there is no gender identity. There is only a schedule for the portrayal of gender. (Goffman, 1979: 8)

Performative identities

Although she does not draw on Goffman's work, the insight that there is no (essential, fundamental, foundational) gender (or other) identity also characterizes the work of Judith Butler. Butler, like Goffman, wants to go beyond the harm done by gender relations to an inquiry into the more fundamental question of why the social world generates gendered differences at all.

One of Butler's most important insights lies in her challenge to the hitherto prevailing orthodoxy which proposes that we have a (physical) sex, on to which (social) gender is added, and that while gender is not necessary, we are rather stuck with 'sex'. Conventionally, 'gender' (the playing of a role, the take-up of an identity, the assigning of an identity) has been cast as a set of social phenomena which could be changed. However, underlying this, many theorists suggested, was a biological 'sex' which was based on having a particular type of body. 'Sex' was understood as *not* being social and although it could be changed, this could only be achieved through fundamental corporeal changes (principally surgery).

Against this Butler argues that there is no identity that precedes the social. There is, in other words, no natural 'sex' to which (social) gender is added. Bodies themselves are saturated with sociality, as we give meaning to some characteristics and not to others. She argues that

> The moderate critic might conceded that *some part of* 'sex' is constructed, but some other certainly is not, and then, of course, find him or herself not only under some obligation to draw the lines between what is and what is not constructed, but to explain how it is that 'sex' comes in parts whose differentiation is not a matter of construction. (Butler, 1993: 11, emphasis in original)

Sex and gender are not just internalized (taken on as an identity) but materialized (produced within the material body). This is the point of the title of her book, *Bodies that Matter*. It is sometimes objected that Butler simply ignores the fact that we have bodies and that those bodies have sexed characteristics. On the contrary, however, this is exactly what Butler is concerned with. The very meanings we give to the body – for example, the fact that we understand it in terms of 'nature' at all – are themselves social meanings, and gender is *performatively* produced, at least in part through the body.

Butler takes the concept of performativity from the work of the philosopher J. L. Austin. Performative utterances make something happen. Examples include 'I pronounce you husband and wife', 'I sentence you to five years' imprisonment', and 'I name this child'. In making these utterances, the officiant is not simply making a comment but is making something *happen* (a marriage, a prison sentence, a baptism) the first two of which, at least, are legally binding.

Note, though, how circumscribed this is. It is not enough simply to say the words; certain principles must apply. Austin calls these 'felicity conditions'.[2] 'Felicitous' statements *successfully* bring into effect what they name. Salih (2002) uses the nice example of a clergyman pronouncing the words of the marriage service over his teddy bears. Since there is no legal recognition that teddies could be

---

[2] Goffman plays with this term in his late essay, 'Felicity's condition' (Goffman, 1983), in which he discusses how things come to be felicitously enacted. 'Felicity's condition' refers to 'any arrangement which leads us to judge an individual's verbal acts to be not a manifestation of strangeness' (Goffman, 1983: 37) – that is, the myriad ways in which we act that show other people that we are sane. The essay shows Goffman's attentiveness to the importance of the audience in all forms of interaction.

married, the statement, 'I pronounce you husband and wife' will not be felicitous – it will not 'take'. Similarly, I cannot sentence people to imprisonment even if I believe that they deserve it. If I were a high court judge, I *could* sentence someone to prison, but I could not sentence my children to prison because they refuse to tidy their rooms. So, minimally,

> the person making the utterance must in some way be authorized to make it;
> the place in which the speech act is made must be socially and/or legally recognized as appropriate; and
> the person (or thing) about whom the speech act is made must be socially and/or legally recognized as an appropriate person or thing about whom those words can be spoken.

We need to consider what all this has to do with identity. As I shall explore throughout the rest of this chapter, for Butler identities (and she is most concerned with identities of sexuality and gender) are not *expressions* of some inner nature; rather, they are performed in that they are constantly and repeatedly 'done', and they are performative in that they bring into effect what they name. Furthermore, they are done within a matrix of social relations that authorizes their being done. This is why one cannot simply decide, at will and without consequences, to be one thing rather than another. The social world is divided along gender lines and people are assigned to one of two genders. In certain contexts, it is possible to reassign one's gender (though usually only by accepting a label of psychiatric disorder) but it is impossible legally, and extremely difficult socially, to have no gender at all.

As I have suggested, the performativity of gender is not the same as a (staged) 'performance'. There is no person behind the mask: the mask (the performance) constitutes the person. Butler directly addresses the issue of whether there is a doer behind the deed, a person behind the mask. Drawing on Joan Rivière's theory of femininity as masquerade, she explicitly notes that the mask does not hide, but constitutes, the person. And, further,

> [I]t is important to distinguish between performance and performativity: the former presumes a subject, but the latter contests the very notion of a subject . . . [W]hat I'm trying to do is think about performativity as that aspect of discourse that has the capacity to produce what it names. (Butler, 1996: 112)

Discourses about sexed identities, which apparently simply *describe* a pre-existing state of affairs, are implicated in *producing* sets of social relations in which sex or gender is a significant dividing line; those social relations, in turn, come to seem both natural and inevitable. For Butler, however, they are neither natural nor inevitable: indeed, it is not inevitable that sexed distinctions need to exist at all. Undeniably, though, people themselves make investments in these discourses and often feel rather attached to their gender. The next section discusses the ways in which people come to be positioned (and to position themselves) within such discourses.

Girling the girl: the performativity of gender

At birth (or *in utero*), the very expression of the sex of the child ('It's a girl!') is performative; it positions the child on one side or the other of a gendered divide. From this moment, Butler argues, the child is 'girled' (or 'boyed'). In other words, the child's sex or gender is not inherent in its body: rather it is brought about through this initial speech act, which brings about the situation it names. While it might be objected that girls and boys are born with different genitals, the point is that there is no intrinsic reason to assign the categories 'girl' and 'boy' to the owners of those genitals.[3] There is no *necessary* reason to divide the world up along sexed lines at all.

As the child grows, of course, 'girling' or 'boying' is repeated daily and indeed the child her- or himself participates in it. In effect, she or he comes to *do* her or his own gender identity. This is an example of *interpellation* – a term developed by the French Marxist philosopher Louis Althusser and adapted by Butler. Interpellation refers to an act of 'hailing': Althusser gives the example of a police officer shouting 'you there!' to a man in the street. The police officer interpellates the man as a subject and, in turning round, the man positions him*self* as a subject, acknowledging that it is really he who has been 'hailed'. In turning round, writes Althusser, the man becomes a subject, because 'he has recognized that the hail was "really" addressed to him, that "it was *really* him who was hailed" (and not someone else)' (Althusser, 1969: 163). The police officer here is a metaphor for the law, or for the social rules that govern any given social formation (for example, sexed identity and

---

[3] Intersexed children are an interesting case in point: current medical practice is *always* to assign them to one sex or another. In this case, the 'discursive formation' overrides the genitals – which are supposed to be the basis of the division in the first place.

sexed behaviour). We see examples of attempts at interpellation when politicians make statements like 'All right-thinking people agree with me' or 'As every decent person believes', or when lines are drawn between 'us' and 'them' such that 'they' occupy an untenable position (when 'they' are 'terrorists' or 'maniacs', for example). The form of words involves an appeal to agreement on the basis that few of us want to think of ourselves as 'wrong-thinking' or 'non-decent', or indeed as terrorists or maniacs. In this way we become subjects who are subject-ed to social rules (see also chapter 4).

However, while Althusser was largely concerned with ways in which subjects are *successfully* hailed, positioned and subject-ed by the law, Butler is at pains to point out that interpellation does not always 'work' (we might say that it is not always felicitous). We may, for example, *not* recognize ourselves, or we may think that we recognize ourselves when really it is another who is being hailed. Or, we can undermine the basic premise of the hailing: we can *refuse* to be positioned as intended. And in this, Butler suggests, we can undermine the law that hails us in the first place. This is how change is able to occur.

Nevertheless, such interpellation as sexed beings takes place within an institutional framework that appears to operate on the assumption that this 'girling' or 'boying' will be successful. In other words, the doing of gender takes place in the context of a wider, institutionalized, sex/gender system in which gender both comes to seem natural and derives much of its force from this seeming naturalness. As with Goffman's work, then, it is important to think of Butler's framework for the performative doing of sex or gender as set within a wider social world; it is not voluntary on the part of the subject, nor does it start with the subject. The performativity of gender is compulsory and is set within the confines of what Butler, borrowing from the North American feminist Adrienne Rich (Rich, 1980), calls 'compulsory het-erosexuality':

> It is a compulsory performance in the sense that acting out of line with heterosexual norms brings with it ostracism, punishment, and violence, not to mention the transgressive pleasures produced by those very prohi-bitions. (Butler, 1992: 24)

Rich coined the term 'compulsory heterosexuality' to draw attention to the ways in which heterosexuality is institutionalized (enshrined in state practices, etc.) and normalized (so that it is presented as normal and 'natural', and people are assumed to be heterosexual unless there are explicit markers to indicate that they are not). Heterosexuality is compulsory in the sense that it is sanctioned by a social (and legal) system. It is enshrined in a set of 'rules' that of course can be broken – and indeed there can be a pleasure in breaking the rules. The rules are nevertheless powerful.

So heterosexuality is compulsory and gender becomes a compulsory performance in line with this framework. To consider this further, we have to discuss in more detail the links between heterosexuality and gender.

Compelling performance

Gender, for Butler, only makes sense – only becomes coherent – in the context of heterosexuality. Current social arrangements link gender with sexuality in such a way that they are locked into a mutually reinforcing and defining circle. It is institutional heterosexuality which gives gender its specific meanings, and gender is constructed in ways which enforce and reinforce institutional heterosexuality:

> There's a very specific notion of gender involved in compulsory heterosexuality: a certain view of gender coherence whereby what a person feels, how a person acts, and how a person expresses herself sexually is the articulation and consummation of a gender. It's a particular causality and identity that gets established as a gender coherence, which is linked to compulsory heterosexuality. (Butler, 1996: 119)

In other words, what Butler is arguing is that certain attributes are brought together to establish something we call 'gender'. In the Foucauldian sense, gendered persons, and gender itself, are categories 'made up' within discourses. Further, it is in the heterosexual encounter that gender gets 'consecrated'. That is, gender is given its meanings, its definition and its *raison d'être* through an appeal to heterosexuality. The notion of heterosexuality, we might say, 'produces' – in that it relies on the idea of – two distinct genders which are kept apart conceptually (male being 'not female' and vice versa) in order to be brought back together. In a world without gender, or indeed in a world where genders proliferate, heterosexuality would simply have no meaning (nor of course would homosexuality or any form of sexual identity based on the sex of one's actual or desired sexual partner).

To explain the link between gender and sexuality, Butler (1992) uses the example of the Aretha Franklin song, *You make me feel (like a natural woman)*. The fact that it is possible to feel more or less 'like' a woman (or a man), Butler suggests, indicates the ways in which we only ever approximate the category to which we are assigned at birth. If we are 'natural' women and men, how is it possible to feel more (or less) like what we are, naturally? 'You make me feel like a natural woman' is (presumably) directed to a heterosexual man, who is able to generate feelings of natural womanhood through his desirability and his desire for the woman who is the subject of the song. In other words, *'natural woman' status is established through heterosexuality.* Femininity and masculinity are consecrated in the heterosexual encounter, and it is heterosexuality that gives gender its meanings. But, Butler argues, what if the song were being sung by one woman and directed towards another? What links would then be made between sexual desire and gender? In this, I think Butler is pointing to a rather grudging social recognition of the instability of gendered and (hetero)sexualized identities.

Heterosexuality is constituted as having links with 'nature'; as seeming natural. For Butler, however, it is based on forms of performativity. It is performatively enacted through codes which are normalized, for example through specific types of clothes, make-up, hair (and hair removal!). We might ask why, if forms of heterosexualized gender are so natural, men and women put so much effort into being natural men and natural women.

Heterosexuality, then, relies on there being two different kinds of gendered being. What is more, desire (for the other gender) is understood as, in some senses, *defining* those beings. Femininity is held to consist in large part of desire for men, and masculinity held to consist of desire for women. To be sure, there are subversions of such definitions – and they may or may not be parodic – as with femme lesbians or 'butch' gay men. Subversions, however, indicate the presence of a norm to *be* subverted. Such categorizations are usually guaranteed by reference to 'nature', but, like Goffman, Butler is not very convinced by the concept of 'human nature'. Indeed, and again like Goffman, she argues that there are plenty of indications that such things have to be repeatedly done in order to exist at all. 'Drag', for example, is usually taken as an imitation of an original femininity. For Butler, however, drag simply exposes the performativity of *all* forms of gender. 'Real' women are doing femininity just as much as (though in a different way from) drag queens. Both femininity and masculinity are continually and repeatedly performatively constituted. Just as, for Goffman, we *become* what we continually, repeatedly and compulsorily perform, so too for Butler. Insofar as we 'are' our (gendered and sexual) identities, we become them through performativity.

Melancholy, sexuality, identification

Since, for Butler (as more broadly for Queer Theorists) all identities are unstable, inessential and in need of explanation, she is concerned to explain how we come to make sexual identifications at all. As she notes, it is not possible to read off sexual identity from gender, desires or fantasy. Although these are usually brought together in a unity, it is social arrangements that bring them together, rather than anything inherent to sexual desire, sexual or gender identity and the rest:

> There are no direct expressive or causal lines between sex, gender, gender presentation, sexual practice, fantasy and sexuality. None of these terms captures or determines the rest. (Butler, 1992: 309)

One of Butler's most brilliant and most radical arguments centres on heterosexual identification. Her argument here owes a great debt to Freud, since she is concerned with the unconscious processes which, so far as she is concerned, explain this form of identification. For Butler, heterosexual identifications are made as a result of melancholic responses to loss.

For Freud, all losses – loss of the mother's unshared and undivided attention, loss of the fantasy of wholeness and completeness, loss of the possibility of bisexual love, and so on – are accompanied by psychic mourning. In mourning we unconsciously grieve for the loss we must endure. In his essay, 'Mourning and melancholia' (Freud, 1917b), Freud suggests that the inability to properly mourn – to 'get over' the loss, as it were, leads to melancholia, a kind of pathological continuation of mourning.

By the later essay, 'The ego and the id' (1923), however, Freud saw melancholia not as pathological but as something inevitable in the process of ego formation. That is, the ego develops through unconsciously incorporating the losses it must endure. Freud points to the ways in which various losses – the things we have unconsciously to give up – impact on 'who we are' (not only our sexual identity, but the whole of our psychic make-up):

> When it happens that a person has to give up a sexual object, there quite often ensues an alteration of his ego which can only be described as a setting up of the object inside the ego, as it occurs in melancholia . . . [T]he process, especially in the early phases of development, is a very frequent one, and makes it possible to suppose that the character of the ego is a precipitate of abandoned object-cathexes and that it contains the history of those object-cathexes. (Freud, 1923: 368)

As we lose things in reality, we take them into the ego in fantasy. Freud continues,

> When the ego assumes the features of the object, it is forcing itself, so to speak, upon the id as a love-object and is trying to make good the id's loss by saying, 'Look, you can love me too – I am so like the object'. (Freud, 1923: 369)

The result of melancholia, in other words, is that we *become* the person (or the thing) we have had to give up. Butler uses this formulation in *Bodies that Matter* to explain melancholic heterosexual identification. She argues that the heterosexual woman (for example) *becomes* the woman she never mourned. She suggests that this is a particularly intense process, since the lost object (in this case, women) cannot be mourned – cannot be grieved for – because it is rendered 'unlivable' – it is untenable. For Butler, the lost object (forbidden to be mourned) becomes incorporated into the ego. She writes, 'Melancholy is both the refusal of grief and the incorporation of loss, a miming of the death it cannot mourn' (Butler, 1993: 142).

> The straight man *becomes* (mimes, cites, appropriates, assumes the status of) the man he 'never' loved and 'never' grieved: the straight woman *becomes* the woman she 'never' loved and 'never' grieved. It is in this sense, then, that what is most apparently performed as gender is the sign and symptom of a pervasive disavowal. (Butler, 1993: 236)

For Butler, then, heterosexuality is built on fragile foundations: on the denial of the non-heterosexual possibilities that haunt it. This is a radical challenge to notions of natural, fixed and unitary sexual identities of all kinds. It is, in my view, extremely important and significant in displacing entrenched notions of stable and fixed identities. However, the problem with this formulation is that it does not explain how heterosexuality, as a system and as a series of dispositions, is able to continue. As Jonathan Dollimore (2001) notes,

> [T]he evidence for Butler's diagnosis of the permanent instability, panic and crisis of heterosexuality is the very fact of its survival and persistence. But when demonstrable historical 'success' becomes the main evidence of radical failure, and actual real-world perpetuation the sure sign of an innate possibility, things are getting wishful in the extreme. (Dollimore, 2001: 41) [4]

---

[4] The use of 'wishful' probably needs to be explained. This is part of Dollimore's critique of what he calls 'wishful' theory – that is, theory that 'wishes away' social conditions. He sees this as 'akin to trying to make history in conditions of our own choosing' (2001: 37).

Nevertheless, Butler's account here stands as an impressive attempt to rethink identity in ways that highlight its inability ever to be tied down once and for all.

Concluding remarks

Both Butler and Goffman see identity as done rather than owned, and both accentuate the notion of identity in process. Both challenge the distinction between 'being' and 'acting', since there is no other way to be than to act. It is also clear that, for both of them, the relation between the individual and the social is of primary concern, as they consider what Butler calls 'improvisation within a scene of constraint' (Butler, 2004a: 2).

Butler, however, is clearly concerned, in a way that Goffman is not, with the unconscious processes at work in performativity. I think, however, that the major area in which the two diverge is that Goffman is largely concerned with how the social order works: how, for example, we are successfully interpellated within it. He is concerned, we might say, with how felicitous conditions achieve their state of felicity. As Terry Lovell (2003) points out, Butler's notion of effective agency and political or social change lies in those times when felicitous conditions *do not* work, when people do not become interpellated, when they inhabit 'uninhabitable' positions. Goffman takes social order as necessary and considers how it is made felicitous. He sees social order, however, as always fragile, as always potentially disintegrating, and as needing to be continually repaired. He considers what must be *repaired* to make it work. Butler problematizes the whole notion of social order and considers what must be *repressed* to make it work.[5]

Both Butler and Goffman highlight the ways in which anxieties about 'authenticity' continue to haunt notions of identity. A normative insistence on the authenticity of identity suggests that identity is held to spring from somewhere 'deep within' us and that, when it does not, there is a problem. Yet as their work, in different ways, highlights, the 'deep within us' can itself be seen as constituted through the performances all of us enact every day.

[5] I am grateful to David Chaney for this formulation.

7 The hidden privileges of identity: on being middle class

Introduction

During summer 2000 and in January 2001, two sets of political protests occurred in the south of England. Both involved parents (mainly mothers) protesting against the housing of child sex abusers within their communities. This issue came to the forefront of British political discussion following the highly publicized disappearance and murder of eight-year-old Sarah Payne, and against the background of the introduction into US federal law of 'Megan's law', a law which allows local residents access to information about registered sex offenders in the area. The protests took place at a time when many were arguing for similar legislation in the United Kingdom. My discussion of the case centres, however, not on the demands of the protests themselves, but on how the protests were represented in the national broadsheet press. In particular, I am concerned with how class circulated within these representations, and with how the protestors' identities were marked in class terms. Class, as I shall argue, is not only found in 'external', objective markers such as employment and housing, but becomes part of who we are – with significant consequences.

Two protests

The first protests occurred in Paulsgrove, Portsmouth, on a working-class housing estate. They were part of a series of protests which took place in the wake of a 'name and shame' campaign run by the British tabloid, the *News of the World*. This campaign involved the paper printing the photographs and personal details of 'known paedophiles' living in Britain. Protestors in Paulsgrove were demanding the removal from the area of men believed to have abused children.

The second set of protests took place in the middle-class London suburb of Balham, and were mobilized against proposals to open a residential centre for serious ex-offenders, including those convicted of sexual offences against children. In both protests, although men were involved, press attention was focused on women protestors. This aside, however, the difference between press representation of the two cases could not be starker. The Balham protests received minimal press attention, in contrast to the enormous amount of coverage devoted to the Paulsgrove protests. In the former case the women were represented as devoted mothers, vigilant, rather than vigilante (Bell, 2002), and identification was invited, so that they became part of a fictive 'we', who are right to be worried about 'our' children. Press coverage was almost entirely sympathetic, with only two dissenting voices (local residents) reported as disapproving of the protests. There were no references to these women's appearances, their homes or their incomes. The only personal details reported were about their jobs (solidly professional), the ages of their children and, in one case, their title (Lady Cosima Somerset). These protestors were described as 'not rioters, but QCs, bank managers and City traders' (Midgley, 2001), an interesting opposition, since clearly being a bank manager or City trader is seen to preclude being a rioter.

The Paulsgrove protests received massive press coverage, including numerous comment pieces. These women were consistently presented in disgusted and dismissive terms. With the exception of a single half-supportive story in *The Times* (Hume, 14 August 2000), which blamed politicians, social workers and 'feminist academics' for stirring up the riots, not a single broadsheet story presented their protest as a rational or understandable one. Instead, they were consistently represented as a 'mob' with all that word suggests of irrationality and insane pack-following. Minute details of their lives – their income, their past relationships, the ways in which they furnished their homes – were reported. Their bodily appearance and their clothing were described in (horrified) detail. It must be noted that the highly charged negative tones which characterized these representations cut across conventional left/right distinctions within the broadsheets: the left-liberal *Guardian* and *Observer* were just as dismissive of the Paulsgrove women as the right-wing *Telegraph* and *Times*.

The Paulsgrove women were vilified across three main axes: their bodily appearance (assumed to indicate a deeper, pathologized, psychology), their ignorance or lack of understanding, and their inadequacy as mothers. Through this persistent and horrific vilification, their protests (*what they did*) were rendered ridiculous through assumptions of immorality, incompetence and ignorance (*who they were assumed to be*).[1]

What can these press representations tell us about identity? Let me be clear that I do not think that they can tell us anything at all about the subjectivities of the protestors – the ways in which they feel about themselves, understand themselves or represent themselves to themselves. They can, however, tell us something about how identities can be *conferred* on people, whether or not they claim them. As Regina Gagnier argues,

> Subjectivity in its deeper forms may also conflict with objectivity, where objectivity means the convergence of the opinions of others. I may feel like a king but I won't be treated like one at the bank. I may feel like a woman but if I walk like a man, talk like a man and look like a man, I will for all practical purposes be a man. (Gagnier, 2000: 39)

There is a long tradition of representing working-class people as a 'mass' or a 'mob' against which middle-class individuality is asserted, but it is doubtful whether anyone *identifies themselves* as part of a mass or a mob. Similarly, terms like 'trailer trash' (in the United States) and 'chav/a' (in Britain) circulate widely as terms of disgust and contempt, but they are imposed on people rather than being claimed by them. Whatever the Paulsgrove protestors felt like, they had an identity imposed on them which meant that, for the readers of the broadsheet press, that is what they became. Indeed, letters to the broadsheets in question indicated that the readers did feel themselves to 'know' these women, in that they felt able to comment on their motivations and more generally on what we might call their internal worlds – while the women were assumed not to be capable of knowing *themselves* at all. While the Balham protestors were constituted as concerned parents 'like us', the Paulsgrove women were being produced as a type that was threatening, repulsive and horrific. This is where light can be

---

[1] For this research I analysed fifty-two reports from the websites of eight British 'broadsheet' newspapers – *The Times, Sunday Times, Telegraph, Sunday Telegraph, Guardian, Observer, Independent* and *Independent on Sunday*, available at http://www.thetimes.co.uk/; http://www.portal.telegraph.co.uk/; http://www.guardian.co.uk/; and http://www.independent.co.uk/. *The Times* and the *Telegraph* are generally regarded as 'right wing' (or centre-right) newspapers, while the *Guardian, Observer* and *Independent* are broadly centre-left. See Lawler, 2005 for a full discussion of the analysis.

shed on issues of identity. As I shall explore in this chapter, one important way in which class 'works' is through the marking of identities and selves as 'wrong' or 'right', pathological or healthy, normal or abnormal. Although class has conventionally been theorized in terms of status or economics, it is important to recognize that classed *identities* are part of the stakes in contemporary class politics. Working-class people, it is assumed, don't know the right things, they don't want the right things, they don't value the right things. They don't look right and they don't act right. By contrast, middle-class identities silently pass as normal.

This chapter will consider some of the effects of the ways in which middle-class identities become normalized and, in the process, become identities of privilege. It will explore how middle-class identity can be seen to be constructed on the basis of a difference from working-classness. This is important, I would suggest, because while academics have mounted challenges to many identities that are marked as 'normal' – whiteness, heterosexuality, masculinity and so on – middle-class identity is much less frequently problematized. Hence this chapter is intended as an exploration of a privileged identity, in particular of the way in which privilege works through notions of 'normality' and 'rightness'.

As I have already indicated, class analysis has conventionally been concerned with 'external' markers such as housing, occupation, education and so on. However, a growing body of scholarship has explored the ways in which class comes to inhere within identities, so that, as I shall discuss in more detail, an individual's whole value as a person can be judged (and found 'wrong' or 'right') in class terms. It is middle-class people who have the power to define and name what gets to count as the 'right' things, and so to define the terms in class politics. As Beverley Skeggs observes,

> What we read as objective class divisions are produced and maintained by the middle class in the minutiae of everyday practice, as judgements of culture are put into effect. (Skeggs, 2004: 118)

The persistence of class

In the last twenty or so years in the United Kingdom 'the death of class' has been widely trumpeted across a range of academic and political sites. In the United States class has long been held to be defunct as a social category. As Janet Zandy has observed, 'Like a ghost, it is there but not there, mentioned but not really welcomed into the multicultural conversation' (Zandy, 1994: 10). However, as several analysts in both settings have shown, class divisions, class distinctions and class inequalities have not 'died', neither has class ceased to be a meaningful category of analysis. Rather, class has become an absent presence; that is, it circulates socially while being unnamed (see, for example, (in the United Kingdom) Haylett, 2001; Lawler and Byrne, 2005; Reay et al., 2005; Roberts, 1999; Savage, 2000; Skeggs, 2004; Walkerdine et al., 2001, and (in the United States) English, 1999; Gagnier, 2000; Lareau, 2003; Wray and Newitz, 1997; Zandy, 1994). Instead, the drawing of classed distinctions has become displaced and individualized. It is displaced on to individual persons (or families) who are approved or disapproved, considered as 'normal', or considered as faulty and pathological. And because class has conventionally been theorized in solely economic terms and around issues of redistribution, there is little critical language in which to analyse and oppose such moves. Yet class has long been figured in cultural and symbolic terms. Pierre Bourdieu has analysed at some length the symbolic dimensions of class, arguing, for example, that one way in which class is configured is through 'taste'; that is, 'good taste' is taken to indicate an innate 'classiness' (read middle-classness). Indeed, one of the primary ways in which the Paulsgrove protestors were represented was in terms of bad taste. Yet, as Bourdieu has argued, taste is an arbitrary category: it does not refer to anything given in nature, but to social categories. In brief, what gets to count as tasteful is simply that which is claimed as their own by middle-class people.

Expressions of disgust at working-class existence remain rife among middle-class commentators. Such expressions of disgust can tell us a great deal about the way in which middle-classness relies on the expulsion and exclusion of (what is held to be) working-classness. Class, in this context, is conceptualized as a dynamic process which is the site of political struggle, rather than as a set of static and empty positions waiting to be filled by indicators such as employment and housing. It is the result of a historical process in which the middle class became a 'class for itself' through distinguishing itself from, on the one hand, the aristocracy and, on the other, the poor (later to be designated 'the working class/es') (Finch, 1993). Although there have clearly been important social, economic and political changes in both working-class and middle-class life in all classed societies over the last one hundred or so years, my argument here focuses on the relational, rather than the substantive, manifestations of classed existence. In other words, I am concerned with how classes exist in relation to each other. As I have indicated, my specific focus here is on the many expressions of disgust at working-class existence within the media and other public forums. These expressions – cutting across conventional left/right distinctions – have largely passed without comment. Perhaps they pass without notice. Why are working-class people constituted as disgusting in their appearance, behaviour and taste? And what are the implications of such a coding for classed relations? While my focus is on the United Kingdom, there are indications that the argument has a broader purchase than this; in the United States, for example, 'white trash' has long been a label of disgust and contempt (although it has recently been reclaimed as a source of political and academic engagement and rethinking; see Wray and Newitz, 1997).

To illustrate my argument I am using representations from a range of sites – from journalism, popular writing and academic texts. These representations are not intended to stand as a representative sample, nor would I claim that this is the *only* way in which working-class people are represented. Neither would I claim that working-class people themselves occupy an 'innocent' position in all this; there are public forums which allow for expressions of working-class disgust and contempt at middle-class existence. But my contention here is that only some expressions count; only some voices will be heard and taken seriously. This is all about power, but it is a form of power masked by its individualism and the foundational status which gets attached to taste, as later sections will discuss.

What I am concerned with, then, is what is respectably *sayable* within a given cultural formation, what constitutes a 'common understanding'. Pierre Bourdieu terms this 'the doxic'. It refers to 'unthought categories', those things which are so taken for granted as being true that they largely pass without being noticed. Although this cultural space is always contested and never fixed, I want to show the ways in which it rests on a set of shared meanings about what working-class people are (and hence what the middle classes are not, and could not be).

Classes are not homogeneous entities, but there is evidence of a sufficiently shared understanding among what we might call a public bourgeoisie (comprising academics, broadsheet journalists, social commentators and the like) about what working-class people are like to speak about a set of doxic constitutions of 'the working class'. No doubt this is a specific class fraction – one with access to the means of representation – but precisely because of this access, it is an important and influential one. This class fraction broadly maps on to Bourdieu's 'dominated fraction of the dominant class' – high in cultural capital but (relatively) low in economic capital. Little surprise, then, that their expressions of disgust occur around the axis of cultural capital.

The issue here is not simply about middle-class people 'looking down on' working-class people. Such understandings work to *produce* working-class people as abhorrent and as foundationally 'other' to a middle-class existence that is silently marked as normal and desirable. But – and more fundamentally for the purposes of this chapter – they also work to produce *middle-classed* identities that rely on *not* being the repellent and disgusting 'other'.

So let me stress that the argument here is not about working-class people themselves, but about the ways in which they are described and their 'problematic' characteristics rehearsed by middle-class people. As Skeggs (2004) points out, such representations have nothing to do with working-class people themselves, but they can tell us something about the producers of the representations and hence something about middle-classness.

Having the knowledge

What is at issue here are the cultural and symbolic artefacts of class which Bourdieu has metaphorized as cultural and symbolic capital (Bourdieu, 1986, 1993). Cultural capital refers to a specific form of knowledge which, as Johnson puts it,

> equips the social agent with empathy towards, appreciation for or competence in deciphering cultural relations and cultural artefacts . . . The possession of . . . cultural capital is accumulated through a long process of acquisition or inculcation which includes the pedagogical action of the family or group members (family education), educated members of the social formation (diffuse education) and social institutions (institutionalized education). (Johnson, 1993: 7)

Not all cultural capital can be 'traded' on equal terms, however (Skeggs, 1997). It is only when cultural capital is sufficiently legitimated that it can be converted into symbolic capital – the prestige or recognition which various capitals acquire by virtue of *being* recognized and 'known' as legitimate. For Bourdieu, it is only the cultural capital of the middle classes which is legitimated in this way; their tastes, knowledges and dispositions are coded as *inherently* 'tasteful', inherently knowledgeable, *inherently* 'right'. In this way class distinctions are simultaneously at work and obscured: they are at work through the distinctions drawn between the cultural competencies attached to different social class positions, and they are obscured because they become, not a matter of inequality in legitimated forms of knowledge and aesthetics but, precisely, knowledge and aesthetics themselves. Not to possess symbolic capital is to 'fail' in the games of aesthetic judgement, of knowledge and of cultural competence. Working-class and middle-class cultural capital is not 'equal but different'; rather, the 'difference' which working-class people display is *made into* inequality (Walkerdine and Lucey, 1989). This is because 'difference' assumes difference from a norm. Further, because the cultural capital of the middle classes is marked as 'normal', its classed location is obscured.

Bourdieu's analysis is useful here because of the ways in which it both highlights and overturns conventional assumptions about cultural competencies and cultural knowledges. These competencies and knowledges are not usually seen as social mechanisms; rather, they are assumed to be part of the self, and this in itself has specific social and cultural effects. In this sense, then, class is not simply an 'objective' position which one occupies, but becomes configured into 'who we are'.

As Sennett and Cobb (1977) famously observed, class inflicts 'hidden injuries'. These injuries are hidden because they do not inhere in the more visible and obvious manifestations of lack – which may also be present – but in the ridicule, shaming, silence and self-scrutiny which go along with a position of pathology.

Habitus and the subject

Bourdieu's concept of habitus is central to his analysis of social identity, and represents his attempt to theorize the ways in which the social is incorporated into the self. This includes a literal in-corp-oration so that social relations become part of the body – how we stand, how we move, how we look and how we feel. Habitus is a 'socialized subjectivity' (Bourdieu and Wacquant, 2002: 126); it is Bourdieu's way of theorizing a self which is socially produced. It is a way of analysing how social relations become constituted within the self, but also how the self is constitutive of social relations. It has been described as a 'second sense', 'practical sense' or 'second nature' (Johnson, 1993) that equips people with a practical 'know-how'. Habitus is manifest in styles of standing and moving and of taking up space, in ways of speaking (idioms, as well as accent), in styles of dress, and so on (Bourdieu, 1986, 1990). It is not, however, confined to the body, since it also consists of series of dispositions, attitudes and tastes. As such, habitus is a concept which cuts across conventional mind/body splits. It also cuts across conventional distinctions between conscious and unconscious, since much of its force derives from non-conscious elements:

> The process of acquisition [of habitus] – a practical *mimesis* (or mimeticism) which implies an overall relation of identification and has nothing in common with an *imitation* that would presuppose a conscious effort to reproduce a gesture, an utterance or an object explicitly constituted as a model – and the process of reproduction – a practical reactivation that is opposed to both memory and knowledge – tend to take place below the level of consciousness, expression and the reflexive distance which these presuppose . . . [The body] does not represent what it performs, it does not memorize the past, it *enacts* the past, bringing it back to life. What is 'learned by the body' is not something one has, like knowledge that can be brandished, but something **that one is**. (Bourdieu, 1990: 73, italicized emphasis in original, bold emphasis added)

As this quotation indicates, habitus carries the concept of history – both personal history and social, or collective, history. Elsewhere, Bourdieu defines habitus as 'embodied history, internalized as a second nature and so forgotten as history' (Bourdieu, 1990: 56). In other words, we learn how to act, how to behave, what is and what is not appropriate, and so on; but we rarely remember that we have learned them. They come to seem 'natural' – a 'second nature'. We learn, for example, the behaviour which our particular culture considers appropriate when eating and drinking: with what utensils (if any) food is eaten, and so on. In adulthood, we rarely, if ever, have to think about how to do this. It seems to come 'naturally'. This, as Bourdieu reminds us, is because we have forgotten that we learned it. If this is so with something like table manners, it is equally the case with attributes and dispositions that are more obviously classed – such as an appreciation of specific cultural forms. What this suggests is that 'taste' is not innate but learned through the deep socialization of the habitus. Furthermore, what gets to count as 'tasteful' – in clothes and demeanour as much as in art and music – is what the group with the power to name things *as* tasteful decide *is* tasteful.

The emphasis on history can make the concept of habitus appear as the carrier of the weight of dead generations, a means of more or less straightforward reproduction. However, habitus is not determining, but generative. Although reproduction across generations does occur within this formulation, the dynamic character of the social world means that it will not occur perfectly: for example, more or less identical habitus can generate widely different outcomes. The daughter of an aristocrat could become a cleaner, although the fact that this would be surprising – at least if 'cleaner' was a lifelong career move – tells us something about the ways in which generation works.

What is central here is the *relationality* of habitus. Habitus 'makes sense' only in the context of specific local contexts or 'fields'. For Bourdieu, a field is a 'network, or a configuration, of objective relations between positions' (Bourdieu and Wacquant, 2002: 97). They are the 'games' for which 'the rules of the game' equip us. But habitus is also relational in another sense: habitus exist in relation to *each other*. Because habitus are profoundly social, they carry the traces of the lines of division and distinction along which the social is organized. That is, class, race, gender, sexuality and so on are all marked within the habitus. Further, and because these social distinctions are hierarchical, not all habitus are worth the same. Some are normalized, while others are pathological. Habitus clash, as well as class. Part of the 'second sense' embodied in habitus entails a judgement of other habitus. However, only some people have the authority to make such judgements stick. It is not, as Dreyfus and Rabinow (1993) claim, that Bourdieu sees everyone as simply endlessly accumulating social 'profits', but rather that 'profits' are made through the owners of some capitals being distinguished from the owners of others.

What gives habitus its particular force, in this context, is that power is conceptualized as working so that it is not what you do, or what you have, that is marked as wrong or right, normal or pathological, but *who you are*. This is not to deny that subjects can resist such a positioning, nor that habitus may be imperfectly aligned with the field (see Lovell's (2000) work on gender passing and Lawler (1999) for a discussion of 'disrupted habitus'). However, it is important to note that there are some people who, by virtue of their habitus, are able to pass judgement, implicitly or explicitly, on others, and to make that judgement count. Differences between habitus, then, come to be made into inequalities (cf. Walkerdine and Lucey, 1989):

> [A] difference, a distinctive property . . . only becomes a visible, perceptible, non-indifferent, socially *pertinent* difference if it is perceived by someone who is capable of *making the distinction* – because, being inscribed in the space in question, he or she is not *indifferent* and is endowed with categories of perception, with classificatory schema, with a

certain *taste*, which permits her to make differences, to discern, to distinguish. (Bourdieu, 1998a: 9, emphasis in original)

As Hannah, a white middle-class 16-year-old in Walkerdine et al.'s study, comments, class is 'also about taste and about dress and about interests. You can spot it a mile off even though it's not to do with money' (Walkerdine et al., 2001: 38). And Walkerdine et al. comment that

> If Hannah could 'spot it a mile off', it would be ridiculous to assume that the targets of her pejorative evaluations would not also be able to spot it in themselves and others, even if they could not theorise it in the way that Hannah's upbringing had taught her to do for many years . . . [I]n this analysis class is in everything about the person, from the location of the home, to their dress, their body, their accent. (Walkerdine et al., 2001: 39)

To summarize: I have argued that habitus constitutes a 'factor of social difference' (Fiske, 1992) which is also a factor of inequality. It is an important means through which 'large-scale' social inequalities (such as class and gender) are made real, and are also made to inhere within the person, so that it is persons themselves who can be judged and found wanting, and persons themselves who can be made to bear the 'hidden injuries' of inequality. Bourdieu's insights give us a method for considering the ways in which inequalities can circulate culturally, as well as materially. Further, Bourdieu's highlighting of the ultimately arbitrary character of social distinctions (so that, for example, what counts as 'tasteful' is an effect, not of intrinsic properties, but of social relations) gives us a way to challenge the taken-for-granted ('the doxic' in Bourdieu's terms). This is especially pressing in the case of classed inequalities, since class is largely silenced, reduced instead to a voluntaristic emphasis on ways to get the working classes to change (Roberts, 1999; Lawler, 2000).

Disgusting subjects: narratives of lack . . .

Savage et al. (2001) found that people were frequently embarrassed and evasive when discussing class. However, if people are uncomfortable discussing class as a *system*, there seems little evidence of embarrassment in characterizing working-class *people* in the most horrific and disgusting terms. True, they are rarely *named* in class terms. But it is clear who the targets are, nevertheless. Across a range of sites, working-class people are represented as both horrific and mystifying. It is as if a nineteenth-century anthropologist had discovered some unknown, exotic people whose strange ways had to be explained to the 'home' population. Les Back (2002) gives a vivid example of exactly this issue from his own work. Back relates an occasion when he was giving an academic paper on white working-class youth, when he was asked (by an academic) 'Are you going to do the voices?' – that is, present the data in the manner of and with the (local) accent of, 'thugs'. Back continues,

> Had the anthropologist parodied 'violent savages' in his preamble to an equivalent paper, there would have been an uproar and an accusation of ethnocentrism. But for him, working-class south Londoners simply did not deserve to be taken seriously, anthropologically speaking. (Back, 2002: 40)

Not only do working-class people like this not deserve to be taken seriously, as Back observes, but they are assumed to be easily 'readable' to middle-class observers, although, interestingly, unable to know or understand *themselves* at all.

Bodies – their appearance, their bearing and their adornment – are central in representations of working-class people. In the United Kingdom, there are references to shell suits, or to 'large gold earrings [and] tightly permed head' (Gillan, 2000), or to the 'Essex girl' whose 'big bottom is barely covered by a denim mini-skirt' (Greer, in Skeggs, 2003: 2), in the United States, to 'big hair', false fingernails, bad teeth, smoking, too much weight. An episode of *The Oprah Winfrey Show* screened in the United States in April 2006, for example, showed people using markers such as these, as well as the more conventional 'markers' of job and education – to locate people as classed. (Interestingly, this show was entitled 'Inside America's taboo topic', suggesting that class is indeed a ghostly presence – there but unacknowledged – in US culture.) There are national differences, but the point everywhere is the same: that such references, such easy invoking of a few signifiers, do a great deal of work in coding a whole way of life that is deemed to be repellent. In a kind of join-the-dots pathologization, the reader (or viewer) is left to fill in the picture by understanding that certain kinds of clothing, location and bodily appearance indicate not only a despised class position but an underlying pathology. This way of using appearance to signify pathology is evident in this extract from Mark Hudson's memoir, *Coming Up Brockens*, an account of his stay in a County Durham pit village:

> [A] group of schoolgirls was approaching along the pavement. One of them, a tall, brawny girl with a shapeless mop of hair, was directly in my

path. I caught her intent look. She imagined that finally, from some Pavlovian courtesy, I was going to make way for her.

No you don't, I thought. Not here. Not in this shithole.

At the last minute she leapt aside. (Hudson, 1994: 16–17)

Here, as in other texts (see, for example, Morrison, 1997; Dennis and Erdos, 1992), the landscape is made horrific and, in a curious elision, its inhabitants are then made horrific, to such an extent, in Hudson's case, that they are denied the basic courtesy of being given room on a pavement. Similarly, Blake Morrison, in his essay on the boys convicted of the murder of James Bulger in 1992, suggests that the landscape in which they grew up 'must have had an effect'. He can hardly contain his amazement at this (extremely ordinary) landscape. Note Morrison's assumption that the inhabitants of Walton (the area in question) will not be reading his book:

[T]he view isn't enticing: pebbledash prefabs, turn-of-the-century terraces, blackened, redbrick back-to-backs, mock-Tudor semis, low high-rises, unsmoking industrial chimneys. The sea and river mouth are less than a mile away – relief, escape – but they're hidden behind the roofs, only stilled cranes to show for them. It's the better end of town, but Coketown all over again: the school could be a factory, the pub could be an old people's home, the reservoir could be a playing field, the only foliage is the moss under broken gutters and leaking gable-ends. In the distance, the spire of Walton church and a hint of unhoused hills: otherwise, a vista drained of purpose, a blot of a landscape. It must have an effect . . . Robert and Jon have never known anything else. But not noticing doesn't mean a landscape such as this has no influence . . . I wouldn't want to live here. Would you want to live here? People live here. (Morrison, 1997: 66–7)

That stark phrase 'people live here' conveys so much of the astonishment of the middle-class observer that places (and people) like this even exist. Yet for many, many people such places are absolutely *ordinary*. This is not Gin Lane; it is an ordinary working-class area. The gulf in perception conveys important things about the ways in which class is mapped on to place. In many ways this is consistent with the logic of class as classification itself, since, as Walkerdine (2003) notes, from its nineteenth-century beginnings, 'class' as a mode of classification was linked with the mapping of areas of cities in terms of disease and crime. This mapping, in turn, was linked with the classification of the inhabitants of such areas in terms of faulty psychologies which had to be described and 'explained'. So, while this is not a new spatialization, it might be seen to be intensified with the advent of geodemographic software (Burrows and Ellison, 2004) and websites such as upmystreet.com which arguably lend a renewed 'scientificity' to the kind of folk knowledge which, in Britain, frequently signifies class in terms of geographical location (as in jokes about 'Essex girls' and 'Scousers', for example). Specific areas (cast as horrific or repulsive) come to be associated with populations that are similarly understood.

This is why both landscape and inhabitants are so frequently described in terms of lack. But this is not, primarily, a lack of material resources, but a lack of 'taste', knowledge, and the 'right ways of being and doing' (Bourdieu, 1986: 511). For Hudson, appearance and landscape combine in such a way that their (assumed) lack suggests a lack of humanity itself. Although he resists the worst excesses of narratives which posit a golden age, he still presents the white working-class people he observes as exotic specimens marked by a repulsiveness which means that they do not deserve basic courtesy. But, more than this, Hudson's text, like Morrison's, conveys his evident astonishment and horror.

I have pointed to the ways in which the appearance of both landscape and inhabitants acts as a marker of an assumed faulty psychology. But even when the appearance of working-class people is not explicitly invoked, the list of their 'faulty' character traits is endless. They are the young males who are 'weakly socialized and weakly socially controlled' (Halsey, 1992: xiv); in the 1970s, working-class women were 'notorious bingo-women who neglect their children' (Hopkins, 1974: 25), or the parents who use 'cuffs and blows' because they are 'less able to put their feelings into words' (Kellmer-Pringle, 1974: 50). Today they are summed up as cigarette-smoking teenage mothers, rearing children in 'deprived and arid backgrounds of instability, emotional chaos, parental strife, of moral vacuum' (Phillips, in Coward, 1994), and whose children will grow up to be 'socially autistic adult[s] with little expectation and even less talent' (Odone, in McRobbie, 2001: 370). They are the 'new rabble' amongst whom criminality is rife, who abuse and neglect their children (Murray, 1994), the fatherless families who bring chaos to their localities and threaten the whole fabric of society (Dennis and Erdos, 1992). They suffer from a 'poverty of expectation and dedication' (Blunkett, in Carvel, 1998), or a lack of 'interest and support' (Milliband, 2003) which militates against their children's school success. They are over-fertile, vulgar, tasteless and out of control. Above all, they are held to lack everything perceived as having value.

This constitution of working-class existence in terms of 'lack' is now so widespread as to be almost ubiquitous. It informs social policy ('social exclusion' presumes a deficit model, as do discussions of 'widening participation') and is present even in some (though by no means all) analyses which are sympathetic to working-class people. Simon Charlesworth's (2000) account, for example, presents an unremitting picture of bleakness and emptiness, in which life often has literally no meaning. Is this about working-class life, or is it about 'a way of looking at it' (Bourdieu, 2000: 53)? While there is certainly no virtue in poverty, or indeed in being on the receiving end of the forms of cultural violence that Bourdieu and others have detailed, *everything* within these accounts is bleak. Yet as Angela McRobbie has argued, 'even the poor and the dispossessed partake in some forms of cultural enjoyment which are collective resources which make people what they are' (McRobbie, 2002: 136). Or, as Skeggs puts it, 'working-class culture is not point zero of culture; rather, it has a different value system, one not recognized by the dominant symbolic economy' (Skeggs, 2004: 153). While these alternative systems are occluded, there can only be lack; one effect of narratives of lack is that they rob the subjects of such narratives of any moral value. But this is given added momentum by an accompanying narrative of 'decline', discussed next.

. . . and narratives of decline

Narratives of lack are frequently accompanied by implicit or explicit narratives of decline, in which, the story goes, there was *once* a respectable working class which held progressive principles and knew its assigned purpose (which, for the left at least, was to bring about social change). This class has now disappeared, to be either absorbed into an allegedly expanding middle class, or consigned to a workless and work-shy underclass which lacks taste, is politically retrogressive, dresses badly and, above all, is prey to a consumer culture (to which the middle classes are, presumably, immune). In such narratives, the decline of heavy industry – often seen as emblematic of working-class existence – is linked with a decline in the *worth* of the working class. Hudson, for example, going in search of the family history of stories passed down to him, expresses bitter resentment that the present reality does not map on to the place of his imagination. Searching for the past of socialist and progressive solidarity of these stories, he finds only an absence: 'The old ways of resistance and communal enterprise had gone, leaving only a slavish acquiescence at the lowest level of consumerism' (Hudson, 1994: 79).

Retrogression – charges of having 'outdated' political beliefs, for example – is a charge often levelled at working-class people, but evidence for this retrogression often simply rests on claims that they are *common* (see, for example, Orr, 2003) . It is as if owning the markers of 'classiness' – a classiness defined as such by white middle-class people – is enough to indicate progressive attitudes. Indeed, the charge of retrogression is a recurring one and is arguably itself a means of distinction. As Nikolas Rose (1991: 18) notes, the working class are seen as suffering from a 'cultural lag'. And Bourdieu argues that 'not only reason and modernity but also the movement of change are on the side of the governors – ministers, employers or 'experts'; unreason and archaism, inertia and conservatism are on the side of the people, the trade unions and critical intellectuals (Bourdieu, 1998b: 25).

The relatively recent discourse of 'underclass' does little to change this. It may be, however, that the discourse of underclass enables an easier disparagement of the contemporary poor (especially the urban poor). Since they are seen to have fallen from grace, there is an implication that they not only could but should be different. At the same time, the use of the term 'underclass' casts this group adrift from 'the proletariat', who were only ever of interest to the left because of their assigned role in bringing about the revolution, but who have manifestly failed in their assigned task of becoming a 'class for itself'.

Femininity has a specific place in all this. Representations such as those outlined above, while not exclusively targeting women, have tended to focus on women as especially repellent objects. This has a long history: Finch (1993) has noted how a nineteenth-century line between the 'rough' and the 'respectable' working class was primarily drawn on the bodies and behaviours of women, and Skeggs' 1997 study shows how little this has changed over more than a century. Since respectability is coded as an inherent feature of 'proper' femininity, working-class women must constantly guard against being disrespectable, but no matter how carefully they do this, they are always at risk of being judged as wanting by middle-class observers. And this is a double jeopardy, since if working-class women can be rendered disgusting by dis-respectability and excess, they have also been rendered comic or disgusting in their attempts to be respectable. In this, they have frequently been understood as inhibitors to the class struggle so that, as Walkerdine (writing here of the mid twentieth century) points out, there 'was a clear implication that working-class men were the carriers of resistance and radicality, with women often being understood as a conservative force' (Walkerdine, 2003: 237).

But at a time when resistance and radicality are no longer associated with proletarian existence, the slippage from 'working class' to 'underclass' can be seen as a feminizing move. Without an assumed radicality projected on to male manual workers, what is left for the middle-class observer to admire? Public discourse appears to have moved from a focus on a masculinized proletariat to a feminized underclass. Instead of the 'noble worker', we have the 'feckless teenage mother'. Both images are problematic, but the second enables an easier disparagement. The working class/underclass is cast as 'feminine' by being seen as workless (paid work being – erroneously – linked with masculinity) (Murray, 1994) and by a focus on bodily appearance and on reproductive behaviour. This, I would argue, is why there is such an emphasis on women's bodies and behaviour in 'disgusted' representations of working-class existence. But while working-classness might be seen as newly feminized, it is not that 'the feminine' has become newly problematic in relation to class (it has always been so).

This begins to point to some of the ways in which 'decline' narratives are curiously ahistorical. Only a minority of members of the working class were *ever* able to claim any form of identity as 'noble worker'. This designation was rarely available to women; Skeggs (1997) rightly points out that there is little that is 'noble' in the caring work in which many working-class women are engaged. But, more generally, nor does it seem to have been applied to the many working-class women and men engaged in shop work, domestic service, light factory work and the like. Moreover, while participation in certain forms of manual labour was able to be mobilized as a positive and worthwhile *self-identity* for some working-class men (Savage et al., 2001), it would be mistaken to take this to indicate a positively evaluated *conferred identity*. It does not follow from a sense of pride in oneself and one's labour that one will be evaluated in positive terms by others.

Indeed, there is plenty of evidence that a middle-class coding of 'disgusting' to mark working-class people – both women and men – is one that has long existed. While 'the working class' in the abstract may have been admired by middle-class socialists, working class *people* seem to have been a different matter.

To take just a few examples: Finch (1993) and Stallybrass and White (1986) have documented expressions of bourgeois disgust at working-class people in the nineteenth and early twentieth centuries. Ian Roberts (1999) has analysed the many expressions of disgust and abhorrence at working-class people within post-war community studies – in which an avowed 'objectivity' does not prevent working-class people being cast as immoral, lying, unable to bring up their children and suffering from a psychic deficiency – either on the basis of what they looked like or because of their unwillingness to concur with the judgements of middle-class observers. Their transgressions, incidentally, included failing to rigidly toilet-train their children and failing to feed infants 'by the clock', preferring to demand-feed. These practices – condemned in the 1950s and seen as indicating these people's ignorance – are now prescribed by health-care professionals. I am not claiming that working-class people have therefore 'got it right', but rather, that more or less whatever they do is understood to be 'wrong'.

So, while some commentators want to suggest that working-class people have newly become disgusting (in ceasing to be 'noble workers', for example), and while it might seem that the disgust and contempt expressed against them is a consequence of recent changes engendered by working-class people themselves, this is not borne out by the evidence. It seems that working-class people have *always* represented something troubling. In nineteenth-century Britain and the United States, when white racial 'purity' was emphasized, the white working class were continually condemned through suggestions of racial 'impurity' – they were characterized as not white *enough* (Young, 1995; English, 1999). Now that there is at least lip-service paid to racial 'diversity', and perhaps a recognition that 'whiteness' itself might be troublesome, the working class becomes *too white*: in the United Kingdom at least, discussions of working-class people tend to focus exclusively on white people, although working-class people are not, of course, exclusively white. But characterizing this group *as* white, means that it comes to be understood as embodying a racism that is officially condemned (Haylett, 2001). (And of course if racism comes to be seen only as embodied in the white working class, the institutional racism of the state, as well as racism on the part of middle-class people, becomes obscured.)

Similarly, working-class people in the nineteenth century and the first part of the twentieth century were condemned for their violation of rigid gender norms (Finch, 1993; Roberts, 1999). Today, although they are still characterized as over-sexual and over-fertile, they are seen as embracing archaic and overly rigid gender relations (Orr, 2003). For about 150 years, ethical and intellectual justifications for middle-class disgust at working-class existence have sat side by side, forming a neat boundary which precludes any middle-class questioning of their own position.

What has changed in recent years is less the sentiments than the explicit naming of class as such. 'Class' is rarely *explicitly* invoked in contemporary expressions of disgust; instead, the 'disgusting' traits are presented as the outcome of individual and familial pathology. Representations of working-class people are marked by disapproval or disdain, not for the 'objective' markers of their position, but for (what are perceived to be) their identities. Everything is saturated with meaning: their clothes, their bodies, their houses, all are assumed to be markers of some 'deeper', pathological form of identity. This identity is taken to be ignorant, brutal and tasteless. As in eugenically inspired (often retouched) photographs popular at the beginning of the twentieth century (English, 1999), working-class people's actions and appearance are made to *mean:* they are made to indicate signs of ignorance, stupidity, tastelessness. An assumed ignorance and immorality is read off from an aesthetic which is constituted as faulty.

We might ask, then, how working-class subjects come to be marked as so 'disgusting'. Disgust is an under-explored emotion (Dollimore, 2001), and this is especially true of classed disgust. While the classed dimensions of 'taste' have been widely discussed, little attention has been given to the disgust that is aroused when 'good' taste is seen to be violated. Yet disgust is an immensely powerful indicator of the interface between the personal and the social. The experience of disgust indicates par excellence that one is 'in the grip of a norm whose violation we are witnessing or imagining' (Miller, 1997: 194), and this grip is immediately felt within the body – it 'makes one sick' or 'makes one vomit', as Bourdieu says (1986: 486). Feeling so personal, so visceral, it nevertheless invokes *collective* sentiments. It relies on an affirmation that 'we are not alone in our relation to the disgusting object' (Probyn, 2000: 131).

Disgust is a powerful emotion; it is involved in the work of drawing distinctions, and it indicates that the distinctions drawn are not necessarily drawn coolly and objectively, but on the basis of intense emotions.[2] As William Miller notes,

> Disgust, along with contempt, as well as other emotions in various settings, recognizes and maintains difference. Disgust helps define boundaries between us and them, me and you. It helps prevent *our* way from being subsumed into *their* way. (Miller, 1997: 50, emphasis in original)

---

[2] Miller makes an important distinction between disgust and contempt. Although both 'assert a superior ranking as against their subject' (Miller, 1997: 32), disgust, unlike contempt, is never indifferent to its object. Disgust appears to demand a certain visibility.

Space does not permit a detailed discussion of the various ways in which disgust has been theorized (but see, for example, Douglas, 1992; Kristeva, 1982; Probyn, 2000), but it should be noted that various analyses of disgust have indicated that it does not arise out of something intrinsic to the 'disgusting' object. Rather, disgust inheres in the *relationship* between the disgusted and the object of disgust. Further, and as numerous analyses have shown, disgust is bound up with identity: part of who we are relies on *not* being (or liking) the disgusting object. In other words, disgust works to 'push away' others, and, in the process, establish one's own identity as non-disgusting.

What is implied here is a recognition of (and horror at) sameness – that one *could be* like all those who lack 'taste', that one could be otherwise. This is the other side to a classification of taste in terms of personal characteristics: if those who *lack* taste could (and should) be otherwise, then those who (are seen to) *have* taste could, similarly, be otherwise. Hence this sameness must be defended against in the form of barriers between classes. I have argued here that one such barrier is 'taste', frequently manifest in its opposite, disgust, but in a sense this is arbitrary: the point is that it is part of a long-standing middle-class project to distinguish itself as different. Indeed, in a sense it matters little what working-class people actually do, since their role is to act as a foil, a 'negative reference point, in relation to which all aesthetics define themselves, by successive negations' (Bourdieu, 1986: 57).[3] Taste may be unstable: yesterday's 'bad taste' may be today's kitsch. Today's good taste may be tomorrow's bad taste. But this instability does not erase its classed relationality. Witness the ways in which middle-class taste shifts in the face of popularization and mass consumption.

In relating the disgustingness of working-class existence, the story being told is that of middle-class distinction. And this story is built on a collective history. Although taste is seen to confer individuality, it relies on a shared understanding of what taste is. Hence, the 'I am I' of bourgeois reflexive individualism (Giddens, 1994) both disguises, and rests on, the 'We are not them' of middle-class identity making.

---

[3] Although at other points Bourdieu seems to essentialize classed taste by talking of the distinction between the 'taste of necessity and the taste of luxury' (1986: 178), I find his argument that the working class forms a negative foil to the middle class more convincing, not least because of the ways in which tastes shift over time (although the properly 'tasteful' is always owned by the middle classes).

Concluding remarks

I have discussed in this chapter some of the ways in which privileged identities are constituted through a rejection and repulsion of those identities with which they could be compared. In terms of classed distinctions, matters of 'taste' work to mark out the knowing and the unknowing, the worthy and the unworthy, the normal and the pathological. The other side of 'taste' – disgust – comes into play in the work of drawing those boundaries.

All of this suggests an anxiousness and a defensiveness at the heart of middle-classed identities. But it points to a wider issue – that there is an anxiousness and a defensiveness at the heart of *all* identities. Far from being stable, coherent and unproblematic, we might see identities as always built on an edgy repudiation of a variety of 'threats'. While some commentators have argued that such an edgy identity is the result of a 'postmodern' era in which forms of certainty and belonging are disappearing, I would suggest this has a longer history. If identities are based on repudiation of what those identities are not, and what they could not and must not be, then it takes work to produce and reproduce such repudiation; can we ever know, then, that we have done it properly?

All of this also underscores the deeply social character of all identities. Middle-classness (for example) might be formulated on the assumption of individualism, but, as I suggested, it is forged through both an association with others who are also middle-class, and a repudiation of those others who are not. What place for individualism here? The Afterword concentrates on the sociality of identity and considers some of the implications of the suppression of that sociality.

Afterword: identity ties

I hope to have shown throughout this book some of the ways in which identity, far from being personal and individual, is a deeply social category. And this is so not only in its more 'public' manifestations – in the ways in which we might identify as 'women', or 'black', or 'middle-class', and so on – but also in its more personal, emotional and affective aspects, in what is often termed 'subjectivity'. Westerners are used to the idea that there are 'public' and 'private' identities; what is perhaps more unsettling is the idea that there is no aspect of identity that lies outside social relations.

The various chapters of this book have considered different ways in which identities can be understood as being socially produced: through narratives, through kin networks, through unconscious processes, through governance and interpellation and through performance/performativity. The preceding chapter considered one example of identity in action, as it discussed some of the ways in which middle-classness is produced through complex dis-identifications from a working-class other. My aim, however, has been to do something more than showing that identities are socially produced: it has also been to demonstrate that, whatever the rhetoric to the contrary, an examination of the social world indicates that identities are lived out relationally and collectively. They do not simply belong to the individual; rather, they must be negotiated collectively, and they must conform to social rules. So the identity 'Binjamin Wilkomirski' that I introduced in chapter 2, for example, fails in important senses because it is not an identity that has been collectively agreed and validated. The same goes for all the multiple and often competing identities that people claim and inhabit with varying levels of comfort. It is not simply that we are all connected (although we are – and increasingly so). It is also that it is through such connectivities – at various levels – that identities are forged.

'Being made' as a person, as an identity (or, more accurately, a set of overlapping and contradictory identities), throws up troubles; it is perhaps when identity is seen to 'fail' that we see most clearly the social values that dictate how an identity ought to be. Lines are constantly drawn and redrawn between 'us' and 'them', and these lines are drawn around identities such that 'they' embody all of the socially disapproved forms of identity. Disapproved forms of identity vary somewhat according to the context, but their contemporary forms include inauthenticity (not being oneself), dependency and passivity (not being autonomous, not 'choosing'), unawareness of oneself and one's origins (not knowing 'who you are') and being part of a mob (not being an individual).

What underwrites this schema of approved/disapproved identities is a notion that to be a person is to be in charge of oneself and one's actions, to be unique, to be the author of one's life and circumstances, to choose. In short, this is the self of the liberal-humanist or Enlightenment tradition that has come to dominate in the West. Whether it satisfactorily maps on to how social relations are or on to people's perceptions of themselves and their worlds is an empirical question, but I have tried to point to some of its inadequacies. For example, social inequalities of all forms become recast as personal pathologies as the 'problem' becomes, not relations of privilege and inequality, but certain people's 'faulty' identities. Issues of social order become issues of identity.

This in turn suggests that, although identities are seen as 'natural', and although we are enjoined to be 'true to ourselves', it is also believed that people ought in some sense to choose 'good' identities. A gap begins to open up between the concept of natural identity and the very powerful contemporary rhetoric of choice and autonomy.

The idea that we can 'be whatever we want to be' relies on an illusory eclipsing of the social world. Against this, the perspectives I have presented here conceptualize identity, subjectivity, personhood – all these slippery and yet necessary terms – as *embedded within* and *produced by* the social world. The social world *both* produces *and* constrains us as persons. In chapter 5 I introduced Freud's notion of the 'narcissistic wound': the blow to one's self-esteem that comes from realizing that one is not at the centre of the (literal or metaphorical) world. I noted there that Freud argued that there had been three narcissistic wounds visited on humanity: the insights provided by Copernicus, by Darwin and by Freud himself, all of which dislodged the 'special', autonomous status of human persons. Pierre Bourdieu adds a fourth narcissistic wound to this list, arguing that a sociology that takes seriously the notion of the person as a social production similarly challenges the illusion of self-mastery. For Bourdieu, sociology – at least in potential – presents us with a view of persons as both products and producers of the social world. To paraphrase Bourdieu, we contribute to determining what determines us.

As I think this indicates, this does not mean that we are 'cultural dupes'; we are engaged social actors, *doing* (rather than having) identities dynamically through time and space, but doing them within various forms of social constraint. Yet it would be mistaken to see identities as projects which it is possible ever to achieve successfully. As I have suggested at various points throughout the book, they are always bound to fail. Certain identities are held to be normal and unproblematic, but, as Erving Goffman reminds us, few if any of us can comfortably and at all times occupy the category 'normal'. Indeed, and as I suggested at the outset, 'identity' can suggest a coherence that covers over the cracks and fissures in our lives and our personhoods, obscuring the multiplicity of identities we must do in and through our lives. The achievement of identity is creative work and if we are plagued by a sense of not quite getting it right, that is because it is a project that can never once and for all be got right.

I should like to end this book with some comments about the relationship between the collective, social character of identity and the notion of value. As I suggested above, the approval or disapproval of certain kinds of identity draws lines between 'us' and 'them'. Yet such lines mask the ways in which the world, and our identities within it, rely on the interdependence of 'us' and 'them'.

Identity, connection and value

Zygmunt Bauman has noted how the poor and the dispossessed – in current parlance, 'the underclass' – are denied 'the right to *claim* an identity as distinct from an ascribed and enforced classification' (Bauman, 2004: 39, emphasis in original). In other words, an identity is imposed and there is no 'official' space allowed where this may be contested or a different identity affirmed. In 'softer' versions, this group might be designated 'the socially excluded' or (in another context) 'refugees'. 'Tougher' versions when addressing poor whites include 'the underclass', or more insultingly (in the United Kingdom) 'chavs' or (in the United States) 'trailer trash': when concerned with those others who are seen as threatening the nation's borders, 'illegal immigrants', 'economic migrants', or even 'terrorists'. None of these forms of identification depend on those who are designated as such choosing or claiming these identities. Those with the power to name can *identify* both themselves and those without such power. Further, those who are denied any chance to name and define themselves tend to be defined in terms of a 'mass' or a 'mob' and to be contrasted with an 'us' who are defined as individuals. Bauman argues,

> The meaning of 'underclass identity' is an *absence of identity*; the efface-
> ment or denial of individuality, of 'face' – that object of ethical duty and
> moral care. You are cast outside the social space in which identities are
> sought, chosen, constructed, evaluated, confirmed or refuted. (Bauman,
> 2004: 39, emphasis in original)

Individuality, it seems, is not available to all. To be seen as a member of the 'underclass' – as to be a refugee – is to be positioned as without a meaningful identity: simply to be made as part of a 'mob'. Characterizing persons as 'mob-like' divests them both of identity and of value. We can see this forcibly in Giorgio Agamben's notion of *homo sacer* (Agamben, 1998; Raulff, 2004).

Homo sacer is a figure from Roman law: a person who may not be sac-rificed but could be killed with impunity. It is a life utterly without worth. The state's relation to *homo sacer* does not cohere around appeals to self-fulfilment or self-actualization; rather, this is a relationship of brute force. *Homo sacer* has none of the civil rights enjoyed by citizens because s/he has no legal, civic or political identity. Agamben argues that the Jews in the Nazi death camps, illegal immigrants and those detained in Guantánamo Bay and elsewhere under the so-called 'war on terror' are all contemporary or near-contemporary manifestations of *homo sacer.*

Illegal immigrants and 'enemy combatants' are only recognized by the state insofar as they are recognized as having no rights. As such, they are divested of legal, political and citizenship rights. There are significant issues around identity here. Contemporary versions of *homo sacer* are, first, attributed *pathological forms* of identity ('they' are swamping 'us'; 'they hate our freedom'). Then all civil *recognition* of identity is taken away. In important senses, they cease to exist as humans – as lives worth living, as lives with value.

But this divesting of identities reminds us how dangerous it is to con-ceptualize identities that can be forged on the basis of 'us' and 'them'. In other words, identities can be used to draw lines between who belongs and who does not. All kin work draws these lines, although, as we saw in chapter 3, it does so to differing effects. Every nationalist movement does so, as does every word or deed based on so-called 'clashes of civilizations'. In some circumstances it matters more than others. It might not matter if I cannot have an identity as a member of your family (although in some circumstances it might) but it always matters if I cannot have an identity as 'human', or if I cannot have an identity with value.

In chapter 6 I introduced Judith Butler's use of the concepts of mourning and melancholia to explain sexed identity formation. In her more recent work (Butler, 2004a and 2004b) Butler shifts the focus to ask what mourning – or the failure to mourn – can tell us about which lives are seen as worthwhile. In this work Butler gives mourning and melancholia a somewhat different emphasis, and this means that identity is seen somewhat differently. The self that is made up of all those lost others is not explicitly characterized as the outcome of melancholia. Rather, the self which is made up of bits and pieces of others seems to be a necessary, even a foundational, condition for human life. We need to mourn, Butler suggests, not in order to avoid melancholia with all its complex and painful narcissistic identifications, but as a way of acknowledging our ontological indebtedness to the other. Indeed, mourning is a way of acknowledging the existence of the other, of continuing to 'address' them.

Butler's recent work suggests ways to reconceptualize identity in terms of connectedness and relationality, and links this connectedness with questions of value – with the questions, what makes for a human life? and for whom can we grieve? In *Precarious Life* she is concerned to think about the limits of 'the human' in the sense that, as she argues, some humans (those on 'our' side) are seen as more valuable – perhaps more human – than others. 'We' can be mourned for, 'they' cannot; 'our' lives can be protected, 'theirs' cannot. 'They' are (although she herself does not use the term) *homo sacer* – identities without worth.

Precarious Life is a post-11 September 2001 polemic that takes as its target US responses to the bombing of the World Trade Center. Butler wants to recuperate grief in the face of US President George W. Bush's announcement (on 20 September 2001) that the time for grief was over and that action should replace grief (in Butler, 2004b). For Butler, however, grief cannot and should not be done away with so peremptorily. Furthermore, grief tells us something about what it means to be in the world as a human subject, even as it is largely disavowed. For Butler, 'Grief . . . exposes the constitutive sociality of the self, a basis for thinking a political community of a complex order' (2004a: 19). It is in grief (as in desire, or in ecstasy) that we see most clearly 'the limits of autonomy', for when we grieve, we are acting out of connectedness, a sense that not only is the person grieved for *worth* grieving for, but that part of our grief is about the loss of part of ourselves in the other. In one of the most haunting phrases of the book, Butler writes, 'Let's face it. We're undone by each other. And if we're not, we're missing something' (2004b: 23).

What would it mean to be 'undone' by someone? I think here Butler wants to get at a more radical notion of human interconnectedness than even 'relationality' implies. As well as seeing our selves, our identities, as relationally produced – as produced within matrices of social relations – Butler wants to consider the ways in which they are also *un*done. As we performatively 'do' our identities, we are simultaneously 'undone' by those others to whom we have attachments of any kind (and perhaps this is everyone). We are 'torn from ourselves' and 'bound to others'. Every desire, like every loss, is a manifestation of the ways in which 'I' cannot be disconnected from 'you':

> It is not as if an 'I' exists independently over here and then simply loses a 'you' over there, especially if the attachment to 'you' is part of what composes who 'I' am. If I lose you, under these conditions, then I not only mourn the loss, but I become inscrutable to myself. Who am 'I' without you? (Butler, 2004b: 22)

This connection, Butler suggests, is a result of a basic human vulnerability; from birth, our bodies are given over to the care of others, even if that care is not forthcoming. In this way we become (social) persons through a vulnerability to others; we become who we are in a world of vulnerability that is both dangerous and (potentially) delightful, and we carry this vulnerability with us. This 'primary and unwilled physical proximity with others' produces, she suggests, forms of being which are far from individual, atomistic and autonomous:

> I may wish to reconstitute my 'self' as if it were there all along, a tacit ego with acumen from the start; but to do so would be to deny the various forms of rapture and subjection that formed the condition of my emergence as an individuated being and that continue to haunt my adult sense of self with whatever anxiety and longing I may now feel. Individuation is an accomplishment, not a presupposition, and certainly no guarantee. (Butler, 2004b: 27)

While it is far from the case that all humans have the same lives or inhabit the same social or cultural or political worlds, Butler suggests that this 'primary vulnerability' – which we do all share – gives rise to a connectedness that is constantly repressed or denied. Her argument here returns me to the point at which I started the book: that 'identity' is a profoundly social entity, but that that sociality is constantly and repeatedly suppressed, at least in the West. It is through the suppression of that connectedness that it becomes possible to view certain people as having identities without value.

I have discussed Butler's recent work at some length here because it seems to me to be one of the most radical arguments for viewing identity in terms of sociality, rather than as something belonging to individual persons. Although Butler herself does not, and I think would not, use the concept of 'identity', preferring notions of 'selves' or 'lives', in the context of expanded notions of identity – as encompassing all the different, contradictory and fractured ways in which we inhabit the social world – her argument is instructive. We cannot do away with claims to identities: on their basis we make claims to political recognition. But we can, perhaps, begin to see them as forged, not within the individual, but in networks of relations with others, some of whom we shall encounter and some of whom we shall not. In this, we are both made and unmade by each other:

> I am nowhere without you. I cannot muster the 'we' except by finding the way in which I am tied to 'you', by trying to translate but finding that my own language must break up and yield if I am to know you. You are what I gain through this disorientation and loss. This is how the human comes into being, again and again, as that which we have yet to know. (Butler, 2004b: 49)

References

Agamben, G. 1998: *Homo Sacer: Sovereign Power and Bare Life*. Stanford: Stanford University Press.

Allen, G. 1999: *The Sociology of the Family: A Reader*. Oxford: Blackwell.

Althusser, L. 1969: Ideology and ideological state apparatuses. In *Lenin and Philosophy and Other Essays*, trans. B. Brewster. London: New Left Books.

Back, L. 2002: Guess who's coming to dinner? The political morality of investigating whiteness in the grey zone. In L. Back and V. Ware, *Out of Whiteness: Color, Politics and Culture*. Chicago: University of Chicago Press.

Barrett, M. 1991: *The Politics of Truth: From Marx to Foucault*. Cambridge: Polity.

Barrett, M. 1992: Psychoanalysis and feminism: a British sociologist's view. *Signs*, 17, 21, 455–66.

Bauman, Z. 2004: *Identity*. Cambridge: Polity.

Beck, U. 1994: The reinvention of politics: towards a theory of reflexive modernization, in U. Beck, A. Giddens and S. Lash, *Reflexive Modernization: Politics, Tradition and Aesthetics in the Modern Social Order*. Cambridge: Polity.

Bell, V. 2002: The vigilant(e) parent and the paedophile: the *News of the World* campaign 2000 and the contemporary governmentality of child sexual abuse. *Feminist Theory*, 3, 1, 83–102.

Bennett, A. 2005: *Untold Stories*. London: Faber & Faber.

Bennett, G. 2005: Masquerade. *London Review of Books*, 27, 1 (3 November).

Berlant, L. 2000: The subject of true feeling: pain, privacy and politics. In S. Ahmed, J. Kilby, C. Lury, M. McNeil, and B. Skeggs, *Transformations: Thinking through Feminism*. London: Routledge.

Binks, R. 2006: Who do you think you are? Final honours dissertation, SASS, Durham University.

Bourdieu, P. 1986: *Distinction*, trans. R. Nice. London: Routledge and Kegan Paul.

Bourdieu, P. 1990: *The Logic of Practice*, trans. R. Nice. Cambridge: Polity.

Bourdieu, P. 1993: *The Field of Cultural Production: Essays on Art and Literature*, ed. and introduced R. Johnson. Cambridge: Polity.

Bourdieu, P. 1998a: *Practical Reason: On the Theory of Action*. Cambridge: Polity.

Bourdieu, P. 1998b: *Acts of Resistance: Against the New Myths of Our Time*, trans. R. Nice. Cambridge: Polity.

Bourdieu, P. 2000: *Pascalian Meditations*, trans. R. Nice. Cambridge: Polity.

Bourdieu, P. and Wacquant, L. 2002 [1992]: *An Invitation to Reflexive Sociology*. Cambridge: Polity.

Branaman, A. 1997: Goffman's social theory. In C. Lemert and A. Branaman (eds), *The Goffman Reader*. Malden, MA: Blackwell.

Burrows, R. and Ellison, N. 2004: Sorting places out? Towards a politics of neighbourhood informatization, *Information, Communication and Society*, 7, 321–6.

Butler, J. 1992: Imitation and gender insubordination. In D. Fuss (ed.), *Inside/Out: Lesbian Theories, Gay Theories*. New York: Routledge.

Butler, J. 1993: *Bodies that Matter: On the Discursive Limits of Sex*. London: Routledge.

Butler, J. 1996: Gender as performance. In P. Osborne (ed.), *A Critical Sense: Interviews with Intellectuals*. London: Routledge.

Butler, J. 1997: *The Psychic Life of Power: Theories in Subjection*. Stanford: Stanford University Press.

Butler, J. 2004a: *Undoing Gender*. New York: Routledge.

Butler, J. 2004b: *Precarious Life: The Powers of Mourning and Violence*. London: Verso.

Byrne, C. 2005: Take your tough childhood and write about it. The result? Another sure-fire best-seller. *Independent*, 19 March.

Carsten, J. 2004: *After Kinship*. Cambridge: Cambridge University Press.

Carvel, J. 1998: Labour targets lazy parents, *Guardian*, 16 January.

Chambers, D. 2001: *Representing the Family*. London: Sage.

Charlesworth, S. 2000: *A Phenomenology of Working-Class Experience*. Cambridge: Cambridge University Press.

Chodorow, N. J. 1974 [1970]: *The Reproduction of Mothering: Psychoanalysis and the Sociology of Gender*. Stanford: Stanford University Press.

Chomsky, N. 1986: *Knowledge of Language: Its Nature, Origins and Use*. New York: Praeger.

Clark, C. 1998: Discipline in schools. *British Journal of Educational Studies*, 46, 3, 289–301.

Coward, R. 1994: Kids on the block. *Guardian*, 2 December.

Dennis, N. and Erdos, G. 1992: *Families without Fatherhood*. London: IEA Health and Welfare Unit.

Dilthey, W. 1976: *Selected Writings*, ed. H. P. Rickman. Cambridge: Cambridge University Press.

Doane, J. and Hodges, D. 1992: *From Klein to Kristeva: Psychoanalytic Feminism and the Search for the Good-Enough Mother*. Ann Arbor: University of Michigan Press.

Dollimore, J. 2001: *Sex, Literature and Censorship*. Cambridge: Polity.

Doniger, W. 2005: *The Woman who Pretended To Be Who She Was: Myths of Self-Imitation*. Oxford: Oxford University Press.

Douglas, M. 1992 [1966]: *Purity and Danger: An Analysis of the Concepts of Pollution and Taboo*. London: Routledge.

Dreyfus, H. and Rabinow, P. 1993: Can there be a science of existential structure and social meaning? In C. Calhoun, E. LiPuma and M. Postone (eds), *Bourdieu: Critical Perspectives*. Chicago: University of Chicago Press.

Elias, N. 1994 [1939]: *The Civilizing Process*, trans. E. Jephcott. Oxford: Blackwell.

Elliott, A. and Lemert, C. 2006: *The New Individualism: The Emotional Costs of Globalization*. Abingdon: Routledge.

English, D. 1999: Cleaning up America's trash: the eugenic family studies 1977–1926. Paper given at the Fourth Biennial Conference, Class, Identity and Nation, of the Center for Working-Class Studies, Youngstown State University.

Erben, M. 1991: Genealogy and sociology: a preliminary set of statements and speculations. *Sociology*, 25, 2, 275–92.

Eskin, B. 2002: *A Life in Pieces*. London: Aurum.

Ewick, P. and Silbey, S. 1995: Subversive stories and hegemonic tales: toward a sociology of narrative. *Law and Society Review*, 29, 2, 197–226.

Fanon, F. 1967: *Black Skin, White Masks*. New York: Grove.

Finch, J. and Mason, J. 2000: *Passing On: Kinship and Inheritance in England*. London: Routledge.

Finch, L. 1993: *The Classing Gaze: Sexuality, Class and Surveillance*. St. Leonards, NSW: Allen & Unwin.

Fiske, J. 1992: Cultural studies and the culture of everyday life. In L. Grossberg, C. Nelson and P. Treichler (eds), *Cultural Studies*. New York: Routledge.

Forrester, J. 1997: *Dispatches From the Freud Wars*. Cambridge, MA: Harvard University Press.

Foucault, M. 1979: *Discipline and Punish: The Birth of the Prison*, trans. A. M. Sheridan. Harmondsworth: Penguin.

Foucault, M. 1980: *Power/Knowledge*, ed. C. Gordon, trans. C. Gordon, L. Marshall, J. Mepham and K. Soper. Hemel Hempstead: Harvester Wheatsheaf.

Foucault, M. 1982: The subject and power. In H. Dreyfus and P. Rabinow, *Michel Foucault: Beyond Structuralism and Hermeneutics*. Chicago: Chicago University Press.

Foucault, M. 1984 [1983]: On the genealogy of ethics: an overview of work in progress. In *The Foucault Reader: An Introduction to Foucault's Thought*, ed. P. Rabinow. Harmondsworth: Penguin.

Foucault, M. 1990 [1976]: *The History of Sexuality: vol. I, An Introduction*, trans. R. Hurley. Harmondsworth: Penguin.

Foucault, M. 1992 [1976]: *The Archaeology of Knowledge*, trans. A. M. Sheridan Smith. London: Routledge.

Franklin, S. 2000: Life itself: global nature and the genetic imaginary. In S. Franklin, C. Lury and J. Stacey, *Global Nature, Global Culture*. London: Sage.

Fraser, M. 1999: Classing queer: politics in competition. *Theory, Culture and Society*, 16, 2, 107–32

Fraser, N. 1989: *Unruly Practices: Power, Discourse and Gender in Contemporary Social Theory*. Cambridge: Polity Press.

Fraser, N. and Gordon, L. 1994: A genealogy of *Dependency*: tracing a keyword of the U.S. welfare state. *Signs*, 19, 2, 309–36.

Freud, S. 1914: On the history of the psycho-analytic movement. In Freud 1953–74, 14, 1–66.

Freud, S. 1915: Repression. In Freud 1953–74, 14, 146–58.

Freud, S. 1917a: A difficulty in the path of psycho-analysis. In Freud 1953–74, 17, 137–44.

Freud, S. 1917b: Mourning and melancholia. In Freud 1953–74, 14, 239–58.

Freud, S. 1918: The taboo of virginity. In Freud 1953–74, 11, 191–208.

Freud, S. 1922: Some neurotic mechanisms in jealousy, paranoia and homo-sexuality. In Freud 1953–74, 18, 221–32.

Freud, S. 1923: The ego and the id. In Freud 1953–74, 19, 3–66.

Freud, S. 1924: The dissolution of the Oedipus Complex. In Freud 1953–74, 19, 172–9.

Freud, S. 1925: Some psychical consequences of the anatomical distinction between the sexes. In Freud 1953–74, 19, 241–58.

Freud, S. 1931: Female sexuality. In Freud 1953–74, 21, 221–43.

Freud, S. 1933: Femininity. In Freud 1953–74, 22, 112–35.

Freud, S. 1953–74: *The Standard Edition of the Complete Works of Sigmund Freud*, 24 vols., ed. J. Strachey. London: Hogarth Press and the Institute of Psychoanalysis.

Frosh, S. 1997: *For and Against Psychoanalysis*. London: Routledge.

Furedi, F. 2004: *Therapy Culture: Cultivating Vulnerability in an Uncertain Age*. London: Routledge.

Gagnier, R. 2000: The functions of class at the present time: including taste, or sex and class as culture. *Women: A Cultural Review*, 11, 1/2, 37–44.

Geertz, C. 1995: *After the Fact: Two Countries, Four Decades, One Anthropologist*. Cambridge, MA: Harvard University Press.

Giddens, A. 1994: Living in a post-traditional society. In U. Beck, A. Giddens and S. Lash, *Reflexive Modernization: Politics, Tradition and Aesthetics in the Modern Social Order*. Cambridge: Polity.

Gillan, A. 2000: Chorus of fear and loathing swells in the streets of a latter-day Salem. *Guardian*, 12 August.

Goffman, E. 1961: The self and social roles. In C. Lemert and A. Branaman (eds), *The Goffman Reader*. Malden, MA: Blackwell.

Goffman, E. 1967: *Interaction Ritual: Essays in Face-to-Face Behavior*. New York: Doubleday.

Goffman, E. 1974: *Frame Analysis: An Essay on the Organization of Experience*. Cambridge, MA: Harvard University Press.

Goffman, E. 1977: The arrangement between the sexes. *Theory and Society*, 4, 301–31.

Goffman, E. 1979 [1977]: *Gender Advertisements: Studies in the Anthropology of Visual Communication*. New York: Harper & Row.

Goffman, E. 1983: Felicity's condition. *American Journal of Sociology*, 89, 1, 1–51.

Goffman, E. 1990 [1959]: *The Presentation of Self in Everyday Life*. Harmondsworth: Penguin Books.

Gross, A. S. and Hoffman, M. J. 2004: Memory, authority and identity: Holocaust studies in light of the Wilkomirski debate. *Biography*, 27, 1, 25–47.

Hacking, I. 1986: The archaeology of Foucault. In D. Couzens Hoy (ed.), *Foucault: A Critical Reader*. Oxford: Blackwell.

Hacking, I. 1994: Memoro-politics, trauma and the soul, *History of the Human Sciences* 7, 2, 29–52.

Hacking, I. 1995: *Rewriting the Soul: Multiple Personality and the Science of Memory*. Princeton, NJ: Princeton University Press.

Hacking, I. 2004: Between Michel Foucault and Erving Goffman: between discourse in the abstract and face-to-face interaction. *Economy and Society*, 33, 3, 277–302.

Hackstaff, K. 2004: Genealogy as social memory: making the public personal. Paper presented at Social Memory conference, New School for Social Research, New York. Available at http://www.new school.edu/gf/historymatters/papers/KarlaHackstaff. pdf.

Haimes, E. 2003: Embodied spaces, social places and Bourdieu: locating and dislocating the child in family relationships. *Body and Society*, 9, 1, 11–33.

Hall, S. 1996: Who needs identity? In S. Hall and P. du Gay (eds), *Questions of Cultural Identity*. London: Sage.

Halsey, A. H. 1992: Foreword. In Dennis and Erdos.

Haraway, D. 1991: *Simians, Cyborgs and Women: The Reinvention of Nature*. London: Free Association Books.

Haraway, D. 1997: *Modest_Witness@Second_Millenium. FemaleMan©_Meets_ OncoMouse™*. New York: Routledge.

Hardy, B. 1975: *Tellers and Listeners: The Narrative Imagination*. London: Athlone Press.

Haylett, C. 2001: Illegitimate subjects? Abject whites, neoliberal modernisation, and middle-class multiculturalism. *Society and Space*, 19, 351–70.

Hazleden, R. 2003: Love yourself: the relationship of the self with itself in popular self-help texts. *Journal of Sociology*, 39, 4, 413–28.

Hazleden, R. 2004: The pathology of love in relationship manuals. *Sociological Review*, 52, 2, 201–17.

Home Office/DCA/Youth Justice Board 2004: Parenting orders and contracts for criminal conduct or anti-social behaviour. Available at http://www.yjb.gov.uk/nr/rdonlyres/fa6e1299-84c1-4544-96c8-8f31304c25e6/o/parenting orderguidance25Feb2004.pdf).

hooks, b. 1990: *Yearning: Race, Gender and Cultural Politics*. Boston: South End Press.

Hopkins, G. 1974: *The Moving Staircase: Sunderland 1939–1972*. Sunderland: Wearside Printing.

Hudson, M. 1994: *Coming Back Brockens: A Year in a Mining Village*. London: Jonathan Cape.

Hume, M. 2000: The vilest mob hatred isn't in Paulsgrove, it's in Westminster. *The Times*, 14 August.

Ignatieff, M. 1994: *Blood and Belonging: Journeys into the New Nationalism*. London: Vintage.

Ingleby, D. 1985: Professionals as socialisers: the 'psy complex'. In A. Scull and S. Spitzer (eds), *Research in Law, Deviance and Social Control, 7*. New York: Jai Press.

Inglis, T. 2003: *Truth, Power and Lies: Irish Society and the Case of the Kerry Babies*. Dublin: University College Dublin Press.

Jackson, M. 2002: The exterminating angel: reflections on violence and inter-subjective reason. *Focaal, European Journal of Anthropology*, 39, 137–48.

James, A., Jenks, C. and Prout, A. 1998: *Theorizing Childhood*. Cambridge: Polity.

Jenks, C. 1996: *Childhood*. London: Routledge.

Johnson, R. 1993: Editor's Introduction. In P. Bourdieu, *The Field of Cultural Production: Essays on Art and Literature*, ed. and introduced R. Johnson. Cambridge: Polity Press.

Kearney, R. 2002: *On Stories*. London: Routledge.

Kearney, R. 2004: *On Paul Ricoeur: The Owl of Minerva*. Aldershot: Ashgate.

Kellmer Pringle, M. 1987 [1974]: Ten child care commandments. In M. Kellmer Pringle, *Putting Children First: A Volume in Honour of Mia Kellmer Pringle*, ed. I. Vallender and K. Fogelman. Lewes: Falmer Press.

Klein, M. 1932: *The Psycho-Analysis of Children*. London: Hogarth Press and the Institute of Psychoanalysis.

Klein, M. 1962 [1957]: *Envy and Gratitude*. London: Tavistock.

Kristeva, J. 1982: *Powers of Horror: An Essay on Abjection*, trans. L. S. Roudiez. New York: Columbia University Press.

Lareau, A. 2003: *Unequal Childhoods: Class, Race, and Family Life*. Berkeley: University of California Press.

Lasch, C. 1991: *The Culture of Narcissism: American Life in an Age of Diminishing Expectations*. New York: W. W. Norton.

Lash, S. 1994: Reflexivity and its doubles: structure, aesthetics, community. In U. Beck, A. Giddens and S. Lash, *Reflexive Modernization: Politics, Tradition and Aesthetics in the Modern Social Order*. Cambridge: Polity.

Lawler, S. 1999: Getting out and getting away: women's narratives of class mobility. *Feminist Review*, 63, 3–24.

Lawler, S. 2000: *Mothering the Self: Mothers, Daughters, Subjects*. London: Routledge.

Lawler, S. 2005: Rules of engagement: habitus, class and resistance. In L. Adkins and B. Skeggs (eds), *Feminism After Bourdieu*. Oxford: Blackwell.

Lawler, S. 2008: Stories in the social world. In M. Pickering (ed.), *Research in Cultural Studies*. Edinburgh: Edinburgh University Press.

Lawler, S. and Byrne, D. (eds) 2005: Class, Culture and Identity. Special issue of *Sociology*, 29, 5.

Lemert, C. 1997: Goffman. In C. Lemert and A. Branaman (eds), *The Goffman Reader*. Malden, MA: Blackwell.

Lifton, B. 1994: *Journey of the Adopted Self: A Quest for Wholeness*. New York: Basic Books.

Lovell, T. 2000: Thinking feminism with and against Bourdieu. *Feminist Theory*, 1, 1, 11–32.

Lovell, T. 2003: Resisting with authority: historical specificity, agency and the performative self. *Theory, Culture and Society*, 20, 1, 1–17.

McNay, L. 2000: *Gender and Agency: Reconfiguring the Subject in Feminist and Social Theory*. Cambridge: Polity.

MacNeice, L. 1982 [1965]: *The Strings Are False: An Unfinished Autobiography*, ed. E. R. Dodds. London: Faber & Faber.

McRobbie, A. 2001: Good girls, bad girls? Female success and the new meritocracy. In D. Morley and K. Robins (eds), *British Cultural Studies*. Oxford: Oxford University Press.

McRobbie, A. 2002: A mixed bag of misfortunes? Bourdieu's *Weight of the World*. *Theory, Culture and Society*, 19, 3, 129–38.

Maechler, S. 2001: *The Wilkomirski Affair: A Study in Biographical Truth*. London: Picador.

Meyer, A. 2007: *The Child at Risk: Paedophiles, Media Responses and Public Opinion*. Manchester: Manchester University Press.

Midgley, C. 2001: A very polite protest. *The Times*, 18 January.

Miliband, D. 2003: Birth still determines all in Britain. *Independent*, 8 September.

Miller, W. 1997: *The Anatomy of Disgust*. Cambridge, MA: Harvard University Press.

Minsky, R. 1996: *Psychoanalysis and Gender*. London: Routledge.

Misztal, B. A. 2003: *Theories of Social Remembering*. Maidenhead: Open University Press.

Mitchell, J. 1995: Twenty years on. *New Formations*, 26, 123–8.

Mitchell, J. 2000 [1974]: *Psychoanalysis and Feminism*. London: Basic Books.

Moore, H. 1994: *A Passion for Difference: Essays in Anthropology and Gender*. Cambridge: Polity.

Morgan, D. 1996: *Family Connections: An Introduction to Family Studies.* Cambridge: Polity.

Morrison, B. 1997: *As If.* London: Granta.

Muir, H. 2006: More than 6,500 same sex couples opt for civil partnerships since December legislation. *Guardian*, 8 August.

Murray, C. 1994: The new Victorians and the new rabble. *Sunday Times*, 29 May.

Office for National Statistics: *National Statistics Online*, available at http://www.statistics.gov.uk/ (accessed July 2006).

Orr, D. 2003: Your class still counts, whatever you call it. *Independent*, 31 January.

Park, R. E. 1950: *Race and Culture.* Glencoe, Ill: Free Press.

Phillips, A. 1993: *On Kissing, Tickling and Being Bored.* London: Faber & Faber.

Phillips, A. 2005: Dialogue with Lisa Appignanesi, *Freudian Slips*, BBC Radio 4, 17 March.

Phillips, A. 2007: What can you know? *London Review of Books*, 29, 8, 20–2.

Prager, J. 2000: *Presenting the Past: Psychoanalysis and the Sociology of Misremembering.* Cambridge, MA: Harvard University Press.

Probyn, E. 2000: *Carnal Appetites: FoodSexIdentities.* London: Routledge.

Rabinow, P. 1996: *Essays on the Anthropology of Reason.* Princeton, NJ: Princeton University Press.

Raulff, U. 2004: Interview with Giorgio Agamben – life, a work of art without an author: the state of exception, the administration of disorder and private life. *German Law Journal*, 5 (1 May).

Reay, D., David, M. E. and Ball, S. 2005: *Degrees of Choice: Social Class, Race and Gender in Higher Education.* Stoke-on-Trent: Trentham Books.

Rich, A. 1980: Compulsory heterosexuality and lesbian existence. *Signs*, 5, 4, 631–60.

Ricoeur, P. 1980: Narrative and time. *Critical Inquiry*, 7, 1, 169–90.

Ricoeur, P. 1991a: Life in quest of narrative. In D. Wood (ed.), *On Paul Ricoeur: Narrative and Interpretation.* London: Routledge.

Ricoeur, P. 1991b: Narrative identity (trans. D. Wood). In D. Wood (ed.), *On Paul Ricoeur: Narrative and Interpretation.* London: Routledge.

Ricoeur, P. 2004 [1974]: Psychoanalysis and the movement of contemporary culture, trans. W. Domingo. In P. Ricoeur, *The Conflict of Interpretations: Essays in Hermeneutics*, ed. D. Ihde. London: Continuum.

Roberts, I. 1999: A historical construction of the working class. In H. Beynon and P. Glavanis (eds), *Patterns of Social Inequality.* London: Longman.

Rose, J. 1987: Femininity and its discontents. In Feminist Review (ed.), *Sexuality: A Reader.* London: Virago.

Rose, N. 1991: *Governing the Soul: The Shaping of the Private Self.* London: Routledge.

Rose, N. 1996: Identity, genealogy, history. In S. Hall and P. du Gay (eds), *Questions of Cultural Identity.* London: Sage.

Rose, N. 1999: *Powers of Freedom: Reframing Political Thought.* Cambridge: Cambridge University Press.

Rowley, H. and Gross, E. 1992: Psychoanalysis and feminism. In S. Gunew (ed.), *Feminist Knowledge: Critique and Construct.* London: Routledge.

Rubin, G. 1975: The traffic in women: notes on the 'political economy' of sex. In R. Reiter (ed.), *Toward an Anthropology of Women.* New York: Monthly Review Press.

Said, E. 1991: Michel Foucault, 1926–1984. In J. Arac (ed.), *After Foucault: Humanistic Knowledge, Postmodern Challenges.* New Brunswick, NJ: Rutgers University Press

Salih, S. 2002: *Judith Butler.* London: Routledge.

Savage, M. 2000: *Class Analysis and Social Transformation.* London: Open University Press.

Savage, M., Bagnall, G. and Longhurst, B. 2001: Ordinary, ambivalent and defensive: class identities in the northwest of England. *Sociology,* 35, 4, 875–92.

Schneider, D. M. 1968: *American Kinship: A Cultural Account.* Eaglewood Cliffs, NJ: Prentice-Hall.

Segal, L. 1999: *Why Feminism? Gender, Psychology, Politics.* Cambridge: Polity.

Sennett, R. and Cobb, R. 1977: *The Hidden Injuries of Class.* Cambridge: Cambridge University Press.

Skeggs, B. 1997: *Formations of Class and Gender: Becoming Respectable.* London: Sage.

Skeggs, B. 2003: Becoming repellent: the limits to propriety. British Sociological Association Annual Conference, University of York.

Skeggs, B. 2004: *Class, Self, Culture.* London: Routledge.

Smart, B. 1985: *Michel Foucault.* London: Routledge.

Smart, C. 1989: *Feminism and the Power of Law.* London: Routledge.

Smart, C. and Neale, B. 1999: *Family Fragments?* Cambridge: Polity.

Somers, M. R. and Gibson, G. D. 1994: Reclaiming the epistemological 'other': narrative and the social constitution of identity. In C. Calhoun (ed.), *Social Theory and the Politics of Identity.* Cambridge, MA: Blackwell.

Stallybrass, P. and White, A. 1986: *The Politics and Poetics of Experience.* Ithaca, NY: Cornell University Press.

Stanley, L. 1992: *The Auto/biographical I.* Manchester: Manchester University Press.

Stanley, L. and Morgan, D. 1993: Editorial introduction. *Sociology,* 27, 1, 1–4.

Steedman, C. 1986: *Landscape for a Good Woman: A Story of Two Lives.* London: Virago.

Steedman, C. 1995: *Strange Dislocations: Childhood and the Idea of Human Interiority 1780–1930.* London: Virago.

Steedman, C. 1996: About ends: on the ways in which the end is different from an ending. *History of the Human Sciences,* 9, 4, 99–114.

Strathern, M. 1988: *The Gender of the Gift: Problems with Women and Problems with Society in Melanesia.* London: University of California Press.

Strathern, M. 1992a: *After Nature: English Kinship in the Late Twentieth Century.* Cambridge: Cambridge University Press.

Strathern, M. 1992b: *Reproducing the Future: Anthropology, Kinship and the New Reproductive Technologies.* Manchester: Manchester University Press.

Strathern, M. 1996: Enabling identity? Biology, choice and the new reproductive technologies. In S. Hall and P. du Gay (eds), *Questions of Cultural Identity.* London: Sage.

Turner, A. J. and Coyle, A. 2000: What does it mean to be a donor offspring? *Human Reproduction,* 15, 9, 2019–25.

Tyler, K. 2005: The genealogical imagination: the inheritance of interracial identities. *Sociological Review,* 53, 3, 476–94.

Walkerdine, V. 2003: Reclassifying upward mobility: femininity and the neo-liberal subject. *Gender and Education,* 15, 3, 237–48.

Walkerdine, V. and Lucey, H. 1989: *Democracy in the Kitchen: Regulating Mothers and Socialising Daughters.* London: Virago.

Walkerdine, V., Lucey, H. and Melody, J. 2001: *Growing Up Girl: Psychosocial Explorations of Gender and Class.* Basingstoke: Palgrave.

Weeks, J. 1987: Questions of identity. In P. Caplan (ed.), *The Cultural Construction of Sexuality.* London: Routledge.

Weston, K. 1991: *Families we Choose: Lesbians, Gays, Kinship.* New York: Columbia University Press.

Wray, M. and Newitz, A. 1997: *White Trash: Race and Class in America.* New York: Routledge.

Yngvesson, B. and Mahoney, M. 2000: 'As one should, ought and wants to be': belonging and authenticity in identity narratives. *Theory, Culture and Society,* 17, 6, 77–110.

Young, A. 1996: *Imagining Crime.* London: Sage.

Young, R. J. C. 1995: *Colonial Desire: Hybridity in Theory, Culture and Race.* London: Routledge.

Zandy. J. (ed.) 1994: *Liberating Memory: Our Work and Our Working-Class Consciousness.* New Brunswick, NJ: Rutgers University Press.

Index